SPIRITUALITY AND THE DESERT EXPERIENCE
by Charles Cummings, O.C.S.O.

STUDIES IN FORMATIVE SPIRITUALITY

Volume Two

General Editors:

Adrian van Kaam, C.S.Sp., Ph.D.
Susan Annette Muto, Ph.D.

Spirituality
and the
Desert Experience

Charles Cummings, O.C.S.O.

Dimension Books · Denville, New Jersey

Volume Two: *Studies in Formative Spirituality*

Dimension Books
Denville, New Jersey 07834

First Edition Published by
Dimension Books, Inc.
Denville, New Jersey

DEDICATION

To all who have known the desert experience.

ISBN 0-87193-067-6

TABLE OF CONTENTS

Page

Contents

PART III—CREATIVE RESPONSES TO THE DESERT EXPERIENCE

GENERAL INTRODUCTION

The Christian today has entered a new era of history characterized by rapid change. The time of a monolithic Church civilization is over. The Christian enclaves of medieval Europe will never return. The ghettoes have broken open and we are exposed to other views and forms of life. Faced as we are by a bewildering number of options, it seems difficult to relate them to our inner life direction in Christ.

In a world of increasing choices, we find ourselves often confused about how to grow to our graced destiny in the Lord. The secular world is dynamic, fascinating, seductive. Beguiled as we sometimes are by its grandiose projects, we begin to grow according to its arbitrary enthusiasms rather than growing as self directed Christians in accordance with divine inspirations. We become so adept at reacting we forget how to respond out of an inner at-oneness with the Lord and his word. We try to adopt new life styles, to be in with what is current. We define ourselves mainly on the basis of our occupations and hobbies or on how our neighbors value us. We become our secular roles to gain the approval of the world and betray the Christian in us who has to penetrate and transfigure these roles. We take on new patterns of living, yet we do not try to harmonize them with our spiritual values. We slide along thoughtlessly, bewitched by the media, beguiled by the sophistication of our secular peers.

Propelled by our need for self emergence, in accordance with the times, we forge ahead often in directions that have no real meaning for us because they are at odds with our inner direction. We lose our concrete sense of self and, the more lost we become, the more desperately we search for substitutes. In our desire to emerge and become what we are called to be, we may rush after every fad that offers a quick solution to the spiritual quest.

While present day secular society is a confusion of paradigms and life styles, it offers at the same time an astonishing variety of incarnational possibilities; it enables Christian spirituality to reveal itself in a richness of forms undreamt of before. Because of this pluralism of life styles, more types of Christians can live out their unique destiny; they can find their peculiar niche in the Father's house where those many rooms promised by Jesus are now becoming manifest. We may have lost security and simplicity, but we have gained creativity and pluriformity. The uniform Christian culture may be dead, but Christianity itself seems more alive than ever.

Since it is no longer sustained by a universal Christian culture, Christianity is like a leaven spreading itself through the dough of a redeemed humanity, transfiguring countless cultural styles and forms with the words and wisdom of Christ, incarnating itself in myriad ways in this world. Creative self unfolding in Christ has become a much more personal endeavor. The secular society offers no guidelines for authentic inner growth; only Christ and the masters of the spiritual life, who lived in his light, tell us what is involved in spiritual emergence in dialogue with the ever changing word where he calls us to be his "little flock."

The purpose of these studies in formative spirituality is to contribute to this dialogue. The publications in this series will direct themselves to various dynamics of the Christian life, illuminated for us in scripture and tradition, that gain in depth of meaning when placed in dialogue with newly emerging insights in literature, human sciences, and the contemporary experience of man. Each study intends to help the Christian find his life form in this unsteady and bewildering age. Each intends to help us answer such basic questions as: How can I find my way as a creative Christian in the new, wide open situation of a diaspora Christianity? How can I live the essential message of the faith in my own style now that there is no longer a uniform cultural code to tell me in detail how to incarnate Christ in my life and my world?

Christian spirituality can be seen as a discipline that guides this search for spiritual identity. The words of scripture, the teaching of the Church and her spiritual masters, illumine this pursuit. They inspire attitudes enabling us to be more open to the call of our true self in Christ. Spirituality explores these attitudes; it examines how we prepare for them, how they transform our daily life. When spirituality is approached in this practical way, it is called formative spirituality.

The focus of the formative approach is on the conditions, structures, and dynamics of Christian unfolding in daily life. It wants to facilitate the graced discovery and unfolding of our destiny in Christ. This new field of study tries to establish the necessary and sufficient conditions for our personal-spiritual formation. It examines from this perspective special and personal spiritualities, experiences, devotions and exercises, abstracting in this way the essentials. It attempts to provide the Christian with a lasting foundation for graced living in Christ; it helps him to find his own practical and particular solutions to the life questions he will have to face without betraying the fundamental conditions of a Christian spiritual life.

This approach also takes into account the psychological,

social and physiological obstacles that may interfere with the discovery of our true life form or life direction in Christ. Similar obstacles may hinder the full permeation of our whole life and personality by grace. The human sciences contain findings and insights regarding such obstacles and suggest effective ways of coping with them. Formative spirituality integrates—and if necessary transforms—such insights along with those found in Church doctrine, scripture, spiritual theology and philosophy into a self consistent approach to the personal-spiritual formation of the Christian.

Formative spirituality is in this way profoundly practical, for it refers to what effects a change in the inner life of the Christian. Change of a superficial nature affects mainly the emotional, psychological or external surface of personal life; profound change effects a lasting inner conversion. Formative spirituality tries, therefore, to discover, describe and apply the principles of the process of a profoundly practical change by grace. In this way it wants to be of help to Christians who go through conversion experiences at various successive stages of a deepening of their life by grace.

Formative spirituality builds on a theory of the development of the human person in relation to the invitation of grace. Contributions from such fields as the biblical and historical study of spirituality, the critical-textual approach to spiritual masters, and the systematic theology of spirituality are taken into account whenever advisable or necessary, but they are not the prime focus of this new field, which is to assist Christians in the discovery and unfolding of a unique life form rooted in their human make-up and in the specific direction grace gives to their lives.

During fifteen years or more of developing this specialty, the results have been most gratifying. The vast majority of students, after three years of study and preparation in this field, have spontaneously reported on profound changes they experience in their personality and in the people entrusted to their care. The studies presented in this series have been written by men and women who for a prolonged period of time have participated in the unfolding of the new discipline of formative spirituality at the Center for the Study of Spirituality at the Institute of Formative Spirituality at Duquesne University. It is our hope that this series will enable the reader to participate in the fruits of this new field of study and to become a little more aware of the dialogue and deepening to which each Christian is called.

The Editors

FOREWORD

The second book of our series of Studies in Formative Spirituality is on spirituality and desert experience. It complements well the first book in this series on suffering. The desert experience presents us with the kind of suffering that brings us closer to God.

The desert is first of all a physical place, usually associated with hot sun, dry sand and dust, sparse vegetation. From earliest times, within and outside of Christianity, it has been a place to which people retreated when they sought intense solitude, silence and closeness to God. Secondly, desert is another word for a place of spiritual retreat. This place can be the geographical desert, but it can also be a retreat center, a hermit's dwelling or a house of prayer. Thirdly, and most importantly for the purposes of this book, desert refers to an inner experience of detachment and letting go. In the desert of the heart one learns the true meaning of life. Each of us is a creature sustained by the breath of the Spirit—a fragile, limited being yet one infinitely precious in the eyes of God.

While few of us may have the occasion to go to a house of prayer, while fewer still may ever feel inclined or have the opportunity to go to a real desert like the Sahara, all of us in some way must occupy the "hermitage of the heart" if we want to become truly spiritual selves.

The desert theme appears throughout the Old and New Testament, whether we recall the experience of the Israelites moving toward the promised land or the preparatory forty days of our Lord prior to beginning his public life. For the chosen people the desert experience was God's means of readying them for a more intimate encounter with him. They were his people and despite their recalcitrance and betrayal he would pursue them as the beloved does his bride. For Jesus the time in the desert was spent alone and in prayer. He fasted and faced the Tempter. When he said *no* to Satan's offer to give him earthly power and possession, he said *yes* to the mission the Father had given him to lead all men to at-oneness with the Divine Persons.

What happened spiritually in the desert experience of the Jews and of Jesus? On both occasions the comforts of life are left behind. There are no distracting, soothing pleasures in the desert, only the harshness of life stripped to its essentials. In the desert a man has to fall back on himself; he realizes then how weak and limited he is. It is only when we have deeply experienced and accepted our total helplessness that we may be willing to turn to God in trust and surrender. While the likelihood of our making a trip into the desert itself is doubtful, we too have to go through this experience spiritually. It takes courage to stand alone before God, to leave behind all human support—all proud claims to spiritual greatness—and face squarely the fact that of ourselves we are nothing in the order of grace. We are inclined to be unfaithful to God, to turn traitor, to sin. What an unsettling sight this can be! It means that if we want to come to God, we have to empty ourselves of all self-centeredness. We have to be willing to follow his divine call wherever it may lead, even if this following means foregoing the comforts we would like to maintain in our life.

When we stand thus defenseless in the desert of weakness and sin, when we are faced with the call to total surrender, temptation will come. We hear that subtle voice saying, "You can never make it. That is asking too much!

Don't take the call so seriously. Others don't heed it and they are happy." The crisis of the desert is upon us. Our self protests. Inwardly all is darkness. It seems so attractive to let ourselves be lured away from this emptiness, to forget all about the call to surrender. It might not be so painful were this experience to last only a moment, but the aversion to suffering and the inclination to rebel may go on for days and days. It is the time of purification wherein our pride is being burned away. The experience of our vulnerability becomes so vivid that we have no illusions left about what we can do by ourselves in the order of salvation. We understand then that God's invitation to total surrender is not a stern demand but a manifestation of love, for only when we fully let go of our pride and surrender to him in poverty of spirit can he lead us to true happiness.

The desert experience is thus a preparation for deeper union with God, a means of readying ourselves to cling to him, without whose love and guidance life is only a sad procession of fleeting pains and pleasures. The desert experience brings us to a crisis with which, left to our own resources, we could never cope. But mysteriously, in that deep darkness and spiritual dryness, the God of light and love descends. He sustains our poor selves with his grace; he stays with us until dawn breaks.

In imitation of the attitudes evolved in the desert experiences of the chosen people and of Jesus, we too should set aside time and space—inwardly if not outwardly—for desert-like experiences to deepen our presence to the Lord. In the desert of the heart, we begin to personalize the attitudes that characterized the chosen people in their best moments and that were epitomized by Christ—such attitudes as inner silencing, dwelling with the Divine, patient acceptance of suffering, self-emptying and detachment.

The desert is thus a place away from the bustle of noisy living and large numbers of people. To go there is to be shaken out of the ordinary humdrum acceptance of things and to reflect on their deeper meaning—a meaning conveyed only in solitude and silence. The desert is also a place of prayer as it was for the chosen people and for Jesus. And the desert is an inner ongoing experience of preparing a place in my heart for the coming of the Lord. There I must learn not to complain when things do not go my way—as many of the Israelites did. There I must learn to be content if at times certain conveniences are lacking—remembering that Jesus himself lacked a place where he could lie down and rest. There, in that interior desert, I have to wait patiently and trust that God will give me what I need if I but learn to depend on him more and more.

This dependence demands an emptying of self and its excessive attachment to persons and things; the reward of this desert experience is beyond measure. God himself comes out of the darkness to illumine our hearts with the light of faith; he relieves the dryness with living water that lasts forever. He grants us a gift of divine intimacy that calls for surrender of our whole self—body and soul, mind and heart. To come to live always in the divine presence from that deepest center of self is the purpose of desert experience.

Father Charles Cummings has taken up this theme of the desert experience as presented in the Institute of Formative Spirituality (formerly Institute of Man). In accordance with the integrative research methodology of this new field, he explored in depth and detail what scripture, doctrine and the spiritual theology of the masters have taught us about the desert experience. One of the principles of formative spirituality is to expand on one's own experience

in regard to the theme one is writing about. Father Cummings did so in the beginning of his study and followed up
with a consideration of the writings of present day authors
who touch on this experience in their philosophical,
literary or psychological writings. On this basis the author
was able to confront the religious and Christian meaning
of the desert experience in human life.

We are grateful that Father Cummings was willing to
present us in this book with a selection of sections of his
study that are more directly relevant to our spiritual life.
To be sure suffering and desert experience described in the
first two volumes of this series are not the only themes that
are relevant to our spiritual life. Therefore, we are planning other books in this series that will highlight other
aspects of formative spirituality. They will be based on the
same theoretical-experiential principles that made the first
two books of this series so relevant to people in search of
their unique life form in Christ.

Adrian van Kaam, C.S.Sp., Ph.D.
Susan A. Muto, Ph.D.

Editors

ACKNOWLEDGEMENTS

Grateful acknowledgement is made to the following publishers: Alfred A. Knopf for excerpts from Albert Camus, *The Plague* (translated by Stuart Gilbert, 1969); Confraternity of Christian Doctrine for excerpts from the New American Bible (1970); Doubleday Company for excerpts from Walter Ciszek with Daniel Flaherty, *He Leadeth Me* (1973); Institute of Carmelite Studies Publications for excerpts from *The Collected Works of St. John of the Cross* (translated by Kieran Kavanaugh and Otilio Rodriguez, Copyright 1964 by Washington Province of Discalced Carmelites); Magi Books for excerpts from Jacques Maritain, ed., *Raîssa's Journal* (1974); *National Geographic* for excerpts from Michel Siffre, "Six Months Alone in A Cave" (Vol. 147, No. 3, March, 1975); Paulist Press for excerpts from *The Psalms, A New Translation* (1968, Grail version); United States Catholic Conference Publications for excerpts from Ernest Larkin and Gerald Broccolo, eds., *Spiritual Renewal of the American Priesthood* (1973); William B. Eerdmans for excerpts from Gerhard Kittel, ed., *Theological Dictionary of the New Testament* (Vol. II, 1964).

INTRODUCTION

Have you ever been in the desert? In this book we are going on a journey in the desert. We have all seen pictures of the desert if we have not actually travelled through one. A desolate landscape of sand dunes, waves of heat, sun-baked dryness, perhaps a cactus but more likely no sign of any living thing. The desert is a place abandoned and avoided by living things for the most part. Very few people would choose to dwell in the desert, though some do inhabit areas around an oasis.

The "desert experience" is like living in a desert where there is no oasis. The desert in question is not a physical, geographical desert but a spiritual and psychological reality that can be experienced anywhere and any time, by anyone. I have spent some time in the Sonoran Desert of Arizona, but that is not the desert we shall explore in this book. The desert experience I am speaking of is a phase of our relationship with God, a stage on our spiritual journey to the promised land of God's kingdom.

The physical desert, with its appearance of unlimited, Godforsaken emptiness, is a symbol of the human experience of the absence of God in our life and the feeling of being abandoned by him and left to our own empty resources. The root meaning of "desert" is a land that has been cut off, separated, abandoned. When we speak of a deserted mother or deserted child we speak of people who have been abandoned and forsaken by loved ones. In the spiritual life a desert experience is the feeling of inner emptiness that comes from being somehow cut off from the divine presence that is our deepest satisfaction and fulfillment.

From scripture we see that God seems to have a fondness for dealing with his chosen ones in the physical desert. He spoke to Moses and the prophets in the desert. He shaped a people for himself on the desert journey from Egypt to Canaan. In the desert people are quickly confronted with basic issues: despair or trust, freedom or slavery, life or death. In the desert, perhaps better than anywhere, God can teach his servants the lesson of total reliance on him because there is nothing else for them to rely on.

In the spiritual desert experience not only is there nothing around to rely on, but God himself seems inexplicably absent. We are left with nothing and no one to help us; and our outward desolation is matched by an interior emptiness and hollowness that threaten to destroy all purpose of living. Yet, as we will see, the desert experience need not leave us shrivelled and withered but can be the beginning of deeper personal and spiritual growth. The desert experience, which may last for a long, long time, can be a turning point in a person's life. Whether the experience takes a creative or a destructive turn depends on the way a person responds to it. Traditional Catholic spirituality will teach us that we can survive and grow by creative acceptance of the desert experience, not by resisting it or fleeing from it or stoically enduring it with clenched teeth.

When the desert experience is seen in its inner meaning and accepted for what it is, then we may begin to discover signs of God's caring presence even in his apparent absence. We will try to point out these signs on our journey through the desert. In the desert experience of God's absence we can meet him in hidden forms; his desert presence and transforming power are concealed by a cloud that only the vision of faith and love can penetrate. In Exodus we read that the people of God "looked toward the desert, and behold, the glory of the Lord appeared in the cloud" [Ex 16:10].

The desert experience of the Israelites was their spiritual preparation for entry into God's promised land. They did not choose the form this preparation took; God chose it for them. It is not the desert we choose but the desert chosen for us that prepares and purifies us most effectively. Today there is a healthy revival of interest in the retreat movement. People are seeking solitude in order to deepen their relationship with the Lord and to find the peace and refreshment that will enable them to return to their work with a renewed spirit. These temporary periods of silence and solitude are sometimes called "desert days," "desert retreats," "desert experiences." Something will be said in Chapter Five about the benefits of periodically making a desert space in our life, but our primary concern in this book is the desert experience that is chosen for us and overtakes us in the midst of life whether we like it or not. The desert experience is our spiritual purification for a new life of freedom and love in the land that God will show us.

In Part I we begin our desert journey by considering three common modes of desert experience present in the lives of many Christians and non-Christians today: daily routine, loneliness, and meaninglessness. Part II will hold our contemporary desert experience up to the light of revelation in the Old and New Testament; in this light we will be able to see the inner meaning of the desert experience as a process of purification. Finally, in Part III, we will test our faith-understanding of desert experience against life situations where creative acceptance seems most difficult: middle age, suffering and death.

We shall see how the desert experience, if it happens to

us, can be a passage to a more mature, seasoned, peace-filled existence. At the point in our desert when we feel most empty and deserted it is possible to discover an exhilarating new spiritual energy that comes from a source hidden deep within us where living water springs perpetually.

PART I

EXPERIENCES OF THE DESERT

INTRODUCTION

How do people in our contemporary Western society experience the desertedness and inner emptiness that constitute the desert experience? The following three chapters will reflect on three deserts: daily routine, loneliness, and meaninglessness. Of course there are other deserts. Each person may have his or her own private desert. And what is desert for one person may seem like seventh heaven for another. My desert is the area of my life where it seems as though a tornado has swept through leaving a swath of barren, levelled desertland. And now I live in that desertland with nothing left. There is nothing new that attracts my senses or my mind or my spirit. I never thought life could be like this. "If this is all there is to life, what's the use of anything any more?" And what has happened to my faith? God seems so distant and religion does not seem to make a difference any more. All I can feel within me is emptiness, and a monumental weariness of it all.

The examples and comparisons used in Part I should make it clear that the desert experience can happen in anyone's life and happen in the very midst of life. We can meet the desert in our daily job at the office, our trip to the supermarket, our wait in the doctor's office, our relaxing in front of the TV. Desert experience does not belong to a separate area of our life reserved for exercises of piety but is interwoven in the fabric of life itself for those whom it affects. When I experience the desert, the desert is everywhere around me and within me, and there is no real escape from it. Only by crossing the desert can I reach the other side; but my desert seems to stretch out infinitely into the distance, and the idea of crossing it seems absurd.

It is such a desert we now begin to explore.

CHAPTER ONE

THE DESERT OF DAILY ROUTINE

There are aspects of life that could potentially develop into a desert experience for many people. The constant routine of ordinary duties may turn our daily life into a desert. For most people there is nothing glamorous or dramatic about their typical day. There is no fanfare every time they make a sale, cook a meal, vacuum the floor, teach a class, or whatever they may spend their day doing. Everyday life is full of little, commonplace things that have to be done but do not yield a great degree of satisfaction and fulfillment in the doing. The humdrum of daily life may be our desert.

In a monastic community I was visiting someone asked me, "Where did you get your desert experience to write about?" I could see that he was expecting me to tell him about "My Six Weeks in the Sahara" or some such unusual adventure. He seemed a little disappointed when I answered, "My experience comes mostly from the eighteen years I have lived at my abbey."

I will begin this chapter by reflecting on the desert aspect of my own daily routine of life in the monastery, the routine I know best. Not that everything I have experienced in monastic life has been dry, dreary desert! I am grateful for all the exhilarating times, the peak moments of fulfillment and joy I have experienced. But in the monastery my typical day consists of a routine of activities and duties that are fairly predictable and ordinary. One day is like another, at least in general structure if not in particular detail. The dailiness itself can be felt as a desert.

My typical day is uniquely my own, but in its succession of routine duties it has something in common, I believe, with other people's daily life. The reader will easily be able to transpose my daily experience into the terms of his own life situation. Each person has his own daily desert to cross.

A Typical Day

On an ordinary weekday in January my day begins early, when the alarm goes off at 3:15 A.M. putting an end to seven sweet hours of sleep. There is just enough time to dress, make my bed, and stop at the lavatory before the office of Vigils in church. The tower bell rings and the thirty-five minute service begins: "O Lord, open my lips and my mouth will declare your praise." I glance across the choir stalls at my brothers who have gathered to pray in the deepest darkness and silence of the night. The church is heated but still feels chilly and I cover my hands with the long sleeves of my cowl. The words of the ancient Hebrew psalms rise now from one side of the choir, now from the other, and are lost in the surrounding darkness. I try to make the psalmist's prayer my own: "I am here, O God . . . my soul longs for you like the watchman for daybreak . . . where are you, O my God?"

After Vigils my time is my own, to continue the night watch in silence and prayer. These early morning hours are considered an ideal time for personal prayer and *lectio divina* or sacred reading. I linger in the dark church with my rosary for a few minutes and then make my way up the stairs to the solitude of my room. There I spend the next forty-five minutes in my own Christianized style of zazen or sitting meditation. Leaving my room after this, I seek the refectory, or dining room, for a light breakfast of toast and coffee. Breakfast and washing up completed, there is still time for some *lectio divina* before the bell summons the community to the office of Lauds. Passing a cloister window on the way to the church, I notice that the moon is nearly full today, a bright disc of light in the dark January sky.

We finish singing Lauds around 6:20, and the tower bell tolls the Angelus. I follow the other priests to the sacristy to vest for our community, concelebrated mass. Today is the feast of a twelfth century Cistercian abbot, St. Aelred of Rievaulx, and Father Marius comments, in his short homily, on Aelred's theology of spiritual friendship. As the mass continues I try to enter into the mystery of Jesus laying down his life for us his friends; and I wonder how the friendship of Jesus can be so present sacramentally and yet feel so distant and remote sometimes in actual daily life. After mass I like to remain in church for a quarter of an hour or so of thanksgiving.

As I leave the church, daylight is beginning to illumine the shape of the Virgin in the stained glass window above the altar. The great silence of the night is over, and I hear activity as some of the brothers get an early start on their work. I make my way to the library and look through periodicals for about twenty minutes until it is time to return to church for the office of Tierce. Tierce, Sext, and None are called the Little Hours, and they last about ten minutes each. At the end of Tierce it is nearly 8:00 A.M., and I change into work clothes for my four hour work period. In the distance I can hear a low conversation going on as a couple of my confreres plan their work together.

My own job does not need much planning and I work alone. My department is housecleaning. I have to dust the floors, vacuum the carpet and mats, wash, wax, and buff as needed, empty the wastebaskets, and use the feather duster freely. Besides these regular chores, I have periodic tasks like window cleaning and furniture polishing. A monastery this size keeps me busy, but not so busy that I have to hurry. I can take my time, set a steady pace; it is not a job where I have to keep my mind on what I am doing every minute. I have no complaints about being the housecleaner; I know someone has to do it. But I would have no objections to a different assignment that would be less monotonous. I have been doing this for nearly two years now, and the monotonous sameness of the work is beginning to get to me. I am never sorry when it comes to quitting time and I can put my brooms and dust pans in the closet, take a shower, and forget all about the floors till tomorrow.

Today as I was dusting the cloister, our eighty-eight year old Brother Alfred was peacefully pacing back and forth saying his rosary and getting his exercise at the same time. He lives in the infirmary now, after putting in many long years as cook in the guest house kitchen. He must have found his job boring at times, but at least cooking offers more scope for creativity than housecleaning. As I looked at him I wondered if someday I too will be a white-haired old man pacing up and down these halls.

At 12:15 I am back in the church for the office of Sext. Many are absent because they come in late from work, but enough of us are on hand to hold up the simple melody of the hymn and psalms. After the office we have a couple of minutes for examination of conscience, and then the bell for the Angelus rings, and afterwards we file downstairs into the refectory for our principal meal of the day. The food is plain and vegetarian, but plentiful. We listen to a reader as we eat; conversation is not permitted. The abbot tinkles a bell at the end of the meal, and we begin cleaning up and doing the dishes. Everyone pitches in and we are done in ten or fifteen minutes. My chore this week is to dry the pots and pans after Brother Bill has washed them. As I work I am thinking about the mail I received today and wondering whether I should write a letter this afternoon. I suppose I will; so many people need prayers and comfort.

After dinner those who wish may take a siesta but I seldom feel the need for it. I prefer to go outdoors for a short walk; after working in the house all morning I need some fresh air. It is not too cold today, and Father Benedict has plowed the roads after our last snowfall, so the walk is pleasant. I stop to watch two bluejays fighting over a piece of bread that someone has thrown out for them. All the snow we have had this winter makes life difficult for the birds. The weakest ones will not survive. I guess life is difficult everywhere, even in the monastery; the monastic statistics for perseverance till death are not too impressive. I turn my steps back to the house. At 2:15 I am in the church again for the office of None.

The remainder of the afternoon is reading time for me, until Vespers at 5:30. The first thing I will do is write that letter and drop it in the mail box. After that I can study for a while. Recently I have been trying to learn more about the biblical concept of "glory." The word fascinates me, and when I have studied it I will probably give a sermon or conference on it, or at least write up a memo on it for my future use. Gregory of Nyssa, whose feast we celebrated a few days ago, looked at the whole spiritual life as a progression "from glory to glory." I wonder if Nyssa ever dusted floors for two years. Or am I perhaps losing the perspective of faith that he always maintained?

Around forty-five minutes before Vespers I stop study-ing, do some hatha yoga exercises, and spend the remain-ing time in meditation. Vespers lasts approximately twenty minutes and is the evening counterpart of the office of Lauds. Most of the time I find it easy to pray these offices, supported by the presence and spiritual energy of a com-munity that likes to sing and pray together. Vespers usually leaves me feeling in a serene and grateful mood. After the office I go down to the kitchen for something to eat; often it will be a sandwich of cheddar cheese on homemade whole wheat bread; supper is a pick-up meal available anytime after Vespers.

Supper over, I have about an hour before Compline. The monastery subscribes to the evening newspaper, and I spend a few minutes in the library scanning through it. Father Basil comes up to me and makes a sign that he wants to talk to me. We go to one of several rooms set aside for speaking and there we have our conversation. On other evenings there might be a community meeting during this period before Compline, or a conference by the Abbot or someone else. Otherwise this is a time for prayer and reading, and for slowing down at the end of the day. The final office of the day is Compline, at 7:30 P.M. By now it is dark once more, and Jupiter and Venus are bright points of light in the winter sky. Compline is the office that brings nearly the whole community together in church for the concluding psalms and hymns of the day. We pray for a peaceful night and a happy death; we invoke the protection of Mary and the angels on our monastic community and on the whole human family. The bells ring once more for the Angelus and then fall silent for the night. As the monks leave the church the Abbot sprinkles each one with holy water in a final blessing. I retire to my room, where I read for a very short time and then fall asleep. Silence settles over the monastery at the end of a typical day.

Reflection

In the desert life of the monastery I may experience year after year of such typical days. The seasons of the year change but the daily schedule remains much the same. Every Sunday is a holiday, and there are other feastdays during the year, but the ordinary uneventful workdays outnumber the solemnities. After a certain number of these ordinary days, my enthusiasm tends to wane; the drab factuality of the desert life begins to weigh on me like lead. The feeling of inner emptiness and external drabness is a common reaction to the actuality of monastic life. This feeling is the normal desert experience of the monk. On the level of external events monastic life looks as barren as a desert. Even when the external events are animated by a graced spirit of faith, hope and love, the desert life of a monastery remains a desert life. Even with the highest spiritual motivation, dusting floors day after day and week after week can become a drag. And if the imagination projects itself into the future and sees only more of the same, then spiritual motivation may be tested to the breaking point. When I looked at old Brother Alfred and wondered whether I would go on dusting floors till I was his age, it could have been a bad moment for me, a desert moment. An infinite stretch of pure time seemed to lie before me like a desert, waiting for me to cross it. Work is man's karma, his destiny, but work that is felt to be depersonalizing and mechanical makes one want to throw in the towel from the very beginning. This feeling too is part of the desert experience of the monk. The daily routine of anonymous, humble work is part of the emptiness of desert experience.

I tell myself that the emptiness is spiritually useful, and housecleaning is an inevitable necessity, but the monotony of the work does not go away. I would prefer a more self-fulfilling and creative form of emptiness. Thomas Merton's words chide me when he says:

> We need to be emptied. Otherwise, prayer is only a game. And yet it is pride to want to be stripped and humbled in the grand manner, with thunder and lightning. The simplest and most effective way to sanctity is to disappear into the background of ordinary everyday routine.[1]

I would prefer a more dramatic and heroic mode of purification but Merton is telling me to prefer the desert. He is telling me to persevere in the littleness of life and to love it, to love the obscurity and the hiddenness. Housecleaning is not a glamorous occupation and was never meant to be. Nor was monastic life ever meant to be glamorous. Monastic life is the life of the little ones, of the *anawim* in the pages of the Old and New Testament. As Merton says again:

> For the contemplative there is supreme value in the ordinary everyday routine of work, poverty, hardship and monotony that characterize the lives of all the poor, uninteresting and forgotten people in the world.[2]

I try to live by Merton's program and to sink down into the silent rhythm of monastic life: prayer, work, reading. For a time I am content, but underneath it all there is a persistent longing for something more. I am beginning to understand that this life is designed to be a life of longing, a continual search for the living God who could not be desired if he had not already let himself be found. The monk's heart echoes the psalmist's cry:

> Like the deer that yearns for running streams,
>   so my soul is yearning for you my God.
> My soul is thirsting for God, the God of my life;
>   when can I enter and see the face of God?
> My tears have become my bread, by night, by day, as I
>   heard it said
>   all the day long: "Where is your God?" [Ps 41:1-4]

The psalmist feels his longing like a thirst. And in the desert experience of monastic life the monk knows that thirst. His heart is parched and thirsty with longing until his whole being cries out for the running streams of divine life. Again the psalmist expresses the monk's feeling:

> O God, you are My God, for you I long;
>   for you my soul is thirsting.
> My body pines for you
>   like a dry, weary land without water [Ps 63:1].

The dry, weary earth of my heart cannot live without refreshing water. My longing is for the divine waters to flow gently over the parched earth of my life and bring healing and coolness. I thirst for the divine water that heals and cleanses and restores newness of life. There are times when my thirst may not be very intense, and other times when it becomes extreme, but weak or strong, merely tantalizing or almost unbearable, my thirst is always there and nothing quenches it.

I think God wants me to experience a vital need for him, a thirsty, loving longing that nothing created can satisfy.

He will not let me be satisfied with anything less than himself. He wants to give himself to me like a cup of cool water, even though for a time he withholds himself in the desert. There is a story about a desert father who was thirsty, and lowered the bucket into his well to draw water. When the bucket came up, it was filled with nuggets of precious gold. But the gold could not quench his thirst, and the monk emptied the gold out into the sand. Again he lowered the bucket and this time it came up filled with fine silver. But the silver could not quench his thirst and he flung it away with disdain. For a moment the monk prayed to God, the giver of all good gifts, and then he lowered the bucket a third time. When he drew up the bucket this time, it was brimming with cool sweet water, and the monk drank with gratitude. In this way the monk learned that the thirst of his heart could never be satisfied with anything less than God himself. None of God's gifts can quench my thirst but only the supreme gift which is himself.[3]

Struggle With Boredom

My reflection on the sameness and plainness of my monastic day seems to suggest that the reality beneath the desert of daily routine is boredom. The humdrum life of daily duties can turn to boredom. Life can lose its passion and purpose until it becomes a daily round of tasks to be gotten through in time to begin the next round tomorrow. Boredom and monotony seem to be a general malaise affecting large segments of our Western society regardless of age and economic condition. We can better understand the desert of daily routine by looking more closely at the phenomenon of boredom.

I remember one occasion in Pittsburgh when I was

speaking to a class of thirty high school boys about Trappist-Cistercian life. I began by telling them that our life was oriented towards meditation, liturgical prayer, manual labor, reading, and the continual search for God. I had intended to go on and talk about a typical monastic day when I was interrupted by a question from a young lad in the second row. He asked, "Isn't a life like that awful boring?" Apparently the same thought was on everyone's mind because the class burst into laughter!

There is surely a possibility that any life, monastic or not, where each day is like the day before and nothing unpredictable happens may turn stale and boring. However, the difference between a bored person and a lively, interested person is not to be found in the external situation, which may be the same for both, but in the interior attitude and outlook of each. The external situation, especially if monotonous, may be the occasion and the favorable condition for boredom but not necessarily the cause of it. For a monk may chant the same psalms year after year without being bored, and a dentist may fill cavities year after year without being bored. Things that we love to do never become boring. If we have a loving involvement and interest in life, no two days will ever seem exactly alike. In fact we may occasionally wish for some desert calmness in our life!

But the bored person is out of touch with the truly alive world that others experience. For him life is always the same old thing. He is in a rut and unable to break free of it. He cannot get away from the same old thing. He carries the sameness around with him like chains that inhibit him from freely touching the sources of newness, vividness, aliveness. He may perhaps try something new and different—a new gadget, a new restaurant, a new vacation spot—but to him they seem nothing but variations on the same old thing, and he finds it all excruciatingly boring. A type of gangrene has spread over his soul, for he is alive but not really living. Boredom deadens everything it contacts. The dull, pallid, listless faces we see are the faces of boredom. The bored person is a desert to himself.

Looking toward the future, the bored person can see nothing new coming over the horizon. His future will be no different from his past. He is going nowhere. For him there is only the present, only the interminable now that weighs so heavily on his hands. Time seems to stand still. He hangs in the intolerable empty space between past and future, held bound by his own inertia. He is imprisoned in his desert with no way out.

Part of the pain of boredom is knowing that one is bored, longing to find something interesting, and being unable to find it. What exactly would the bored person like to have? Unfortunately he does not know. Every stimulation he goes after eventually turns out to be a phantom, a desert mirage. Nothing interests the bored person very long. He longs for lasting fulfillment, and nothing satisfies him except perhaps temporarily. Soon he feels that inner longing and ache again. There is an emptiness in his life that is more unbearable than physical hunger and thirst. Bored people will frequently resort to over-eating and drinking in an attempt to satisfy their inner emptiness. But their spirits are hungry and thirsty, not their bodies. The emptiness they feel is very real but not physical. "The bored person is full of emptiness," says psychiatrist Ralph Greenson.[4]

How do bored people cope with the tedium of their life? They often choose one of two responses, sometimes alternating between the two. One response is to withdraw into a state of apathy. When life seems to have gone dead on someone, he no longer cares about anything. He is indifferent to what he does and the way he does it, indifferent to his health and appearance, indifferent to the feelings of others and even their attempts to help him. He is lost in a desert of endless ennui. He is weary of everything, weary of the whole world. Such a person could easily spend the entire day in bed. The victim of apathetic boredom believes that the world owes him a sufficiently exciting reason for getting out of bed.

In the case of the second response a person is inclined to get up and make something exciting happen, or not to go to bed at all. He is the victim of a more restless boredom. He does everything he can think of to avoid idleness and monotony. His days and nights are a frantic search for excitement, stimulation, novelty, diversion. But no distraction, however uninhibited, can permanently relieve the aching emptiness of his boredom. Eventually his effort to stay in perpetual motion, going from thrill to thrill, becomes boring in itself. He finds himself whirling faster and faster but still not getting anywhere. If his speed increases, a disastrous breakdown is inevitable. His life will disintegrate into a handful of pieces that can never be put back together, the broken shards of what might have been.

Is there no escape from boredom of spirit? Not in the direction of things that lie outside the person himself. Only by some inner change, some transformation of mind and attitude, can the bored person hope to find the way out of his desert. For instance, a rediscovery of innate powers of imagination and wonderment can lead to a new appreciation of the ordinary, familiar, routine duties of life. Or a religious conversion experience could revitalize a person's life and bring his daily routine into meaningful focus. With a deepened faith he could perhaps accept the desert of daily routine, remembering that Jesus lived thirty years of his life without acclaim, without fanfare, in a backwater called Nazareth. Patient acceptance will not take away the daily routine, but it may free someone from the desert of boredom. Acceptance has the power to remove all the self-applied and self-maintained shackles that bind a person's spirit and imprison him in the desert of boredom.

Conclusion

The desert experience of daily routine threatens to empty people's lives of all zest and enjoyment. Even a routine of spiritual exercises such as daily Eucharist and breviary can become a desert experience that yields no personal refreshment or satisfaction. Wherever there is routine, there is the possibility of boredom. We have seen how boredom can painfully bind and suffocate the human spirit, preventing it from joyfully expanding toward the horizon of all that is. The longing for satisfaction experienced by the bored person is the longing of the human spirit for relatedness to what lies beyond. To fill his inner emptiness the bored person would have to bore down deep within himself and tap those living sources of identity that lie beneath the desert surface of his life.

A person with an inner sense of his own identity and goal in life has a high tolerance of daily routine. Everything he does is worthwhile because he bestows worth on it. It is not what a person does but what kind of person he is that enables him to rise above the danger of boredom and monotony. I may have to live in a desert of daily routine, but I can have the inner strength to face this desert and take my stand in it with peacefulness and poise.

I may have to spend the rest of my life sweeping the floors, but I can learn to find the highest value in the humblest occupation. I accept the deserts into which the Lord may lead me. The Psalmist expects to be led by the Shepherd to restful waters, but the path to this refreshment may wind through the desert of daily routine [see Psalm 23].

CHAPTER TWO

THE DESERT OF LONELINESS

While the previous chapter on the desert of daily routine brought out the feeling of inner emptiness characteristic of the desert experience, the prominent feeling we will highlight in the present chapter is the desert feeling of having been deserted. Loneliness, as I understand it, is the painful mood or feeling that overtakes me when I am separated from a loved one, or from company in general. I have been deserted by someone very important to me; nothing can replace this loss. In my state of desertedness I am lonely and sad, with a sadness that eats at my heart and empties my life of joyfulness. Loneliness makes me anxious, worried, insecure, and tends to turn me in on myself.

Most of us have probably lived with the pain of loneliness at one time or another in our life. When we are lonely we are inclined to think that everyone else has comforting, understanding friends and we are the only lonely person in the world. We think the desert of loneliness has a population of only one. But there are many lonely people in our world, all trying to hide their loneliness from others and even from themselves by forced sociability and cheerfulness. The desert of loneliness is impossible to cross if we refuse to admit we are in the desert at all. The first step to be taken is owning our loneliness, at least to ourselves. Then we can perhaps begin to understand and deal with our loneliness.

Loneliness comes from a variety of causes and is felt in different degrees. The following sections will survey some common types of loneliness for a better picture of this form of desert experience. We begin with the loneliness that can arise in physical solitude.

Six Months Alone[1]

French scientist, Michel Siffre, endured 205 days of isolation to find out about the natural sleeping and waking patterns of human beings whose schedule is not governed by clocks and calendars. Siffre's isolation chamber had to be situated where he could not observe and be influenced by the alternation of day and night. He selected a place 100 feet below ground, in Midnight Cave, near Del Rio, Texas, about thirty-five miles from the Mexican border. A twenty square yard platform was constructed for his living area and outfitted with almost all the comforts of home. There was good food, plenty of reading and recreation material, and a fixed program of tests and scientific observations to be completed each day. A telephone provided instant communication with the surface crew, but its use was restricted to scientific purposes and emergencies.

As Siffre descended into his solitude the last human face he looked upon was his wife's. For the first third of the experiment Siffre remained in excellent form and was not troubled with loneliness. Then, after the second month, he began to deteriorate physically, mentally, and emotionally. He struggled with loneliness until it became almost unendurable. Only a sense of duty and the hope of important scientific discoveries kept him from terminating the experiment sooner. The telephone, which was a link to the human world above, became for Siffre a symbol of the fact that he was cut off from that world. He wrote: "Far from being a comfort, its presence serves as a malign reminder that I am alone, a captive'' [p. 429]. Siffre was lonely and he knew it.

But the situation went from bad to worse as Siffre gave in to feelings of self pity and despair. On the 86th day he thought of ending it all by committing suicide [p. 431]. A week later he was still hanging on, but he wrote in his diary, "I am living through the nadir of my life. This long loneliness is beyond all bearing" [pp. 431-432]. The human spirit has remarkable reserves for bearing the unbearable, and Siffre held out.

By the 156th day Siffre's prolonged confrontation with his own self was yielding a painful but potentially beneficial insight. He wrote:

> When you find yourself alone, isolated in a world totally without time, face to face with yourself, all the masks that you hid behind—those to preserve your own illusions, those that project them before others—finally fall, sometimes brutally [p. 432].

Solitude and loneliness were leading Siffre to a degree of self-knowledge that few people attain. And the knowledge is never gained without pain.

But a still more painful experience was in store for Siffre. At the end of it he would be at his limit in the desert of loneliness and desertedness. In the fifth month of his solitude Siffre discovered another living creature in Midnight Cave: a mouse. Siffre was jubilant; at extremes of loneliness even a mouse looks like a friend. Siffre hoped to trap the the mouse, which he named "Mus," and have it for a companion. For several days time no longer dragged but passed swiftly as Siffre fed Mus with jam and worked out a plan to capture him under a casserole dish. Then:

My patience prevails. After much hesitation, Mus edges up to the jam. I admire his little shining eyes, his sleek coat. I slam down the dish. He is captured! At last I will have a companion in my solitude. My heart pounds with excitement. For the first time since entering the cave, I feel a surge of joy. Carefully I inch up the casserole. I hear small squeaks of distress. Mus lies on his side. The edge of the descending dish apparently caught him on the head. I stare at him with swelling grief. The whimpers die away. He is still. Desolation overwhelms me [p. 435].

Not a happy ending. If there was ever a moment when Siffre experienced himself as lonely and forsaken, it must have been at that devastating moment when the whimpers of his little mouse died away. The surge of joy and excitement he felt in his heart was stillborn. Siffre had not asked for very much, only for the comforting presence of another living being—yet even that was denied him. Michel Siffre was not living in the physical desert but he knew the full dereliction of the desert experience in the silence and solitude of Midnight Cave.

Prolonged isolation is often the occasion, or the facilitating condition, for the desert experience of loneliness. On the other hand, generations of saintly Christian hermits bear witness to the fact that isolation can be beneficial and productive instead of lonely and sad. Not many people, however, will choose the hermit's solitude or the scientist's cave. These are extreme situations that permit us to study the desert of loneliness in all its clarity. There are many other life-situations where people experience the desert of loneliness, and these we can mention briefly. The "Lonely Hearts Club" has a membership that comes from all classes and ages.

Lonely Hearts Club

The people we will see in this section do not live in physical solitude. They live with other people, yet they may be acutely lonely, deserted people. It is possible to be lonely in the midst of a crowd, both a crowd of strangers and a crowd of acquaintances. The lonely person misses his beloved. There are lonely people in Times Square, despite the crowds. Philosopher Henry Bugbee has said: " . . . New York City has seemed to me the epitome of a lonely place."[2] Any large city may be a desert of loneliness if there is an absence of personal relatedness and loving concern.

Lonely children. Children can experience loneliness keenly. Orphaned children who grow up in public institutions miss the affection of their parents and have to either suffer in loneliness or find substitute parental affection from the staff or from their peers. To a lesser degree loneliness may afflict the children of broken homes who live with one parent and rarely if ever see the other parent. Even infants may feel loneliness without being able to name what they feel. The infant's world includes little more than its mother. When mother leaves the infant, even to go into another room for a moment, the infant has no way of knowing that mother will ever be back. It can feel terribly deserted and alone. Psychologist Clark Moustakas records the poignant case of a little child brought to the hospital by his parents. After reassuring the boy as best they could, the parents left. He was too young to understand what was happening; he was afraid his parents would never return. He sat in the middle of his bed and cried inconsolably with loneliness. As Moustakas watched the scene, his heart went out to the little fellow. He described the child:

> Waiting for someone to rescue him from abandonment. Waiting. There was no one. He was alone—totally, utterly alone. . . . I knew in that moment he experienced a crushing loneliness, a feeling of being deserted and forsaken.[3]

This child wept on his bed in the desert of loneliness where "there was no one" to befriend him; the ones he had depended on had deserted him. Perhaps we carry with us even as adults the residue of our infantile terror of being left alone.

Lonely adolescents. Teen-agers we might see standing around in groups talking earnestly and laughing frequently would not appear to be lonely people. They are able to conceal their loneliness quite cleverly. They huddle together in small groups or large gangs to escape the desert of loneliness that seems to threaten them so frequently. Anyone who may be excluded from group membership, or anyone who may not have a steady boyfriend or girlfriend, is likely to feel very much alone. Peer affirmation and acceptance is critically important to the adolescent, and often spurs him to excel in competitive sports, or attempt reckless acts of bravado, or experiment with drugs, alcohol, cigarettes, sex. The adolescent is lonely because he does not yet know where he belongs in life. He is choosing his life-direction and searching for the standards, values, and goals that will give shape to his existence. Adolescence is a time for defining one's identity, and this is a task that no one else can do, a lonely task.

Loneliness in marriage. Perhaps we might expect to find

loneliness in the lives of people who have never married and who come home day after day to an empty apartment. But many married people are lonely too. The mother may be the first to feel it, when her children have grown up and she is left presiding over an empty nest. The father may not feel it until he retires from work. The couple still has each other, but something may prevent them from discovering each other as friends and so they grow old together in loneliness. Also, in the course of their married life there may be shorter or longer periods when husband and wife may be separated because of business obligations or the like. Separation can mean loneliness in these cases. Then there are marriages that are lonely because loveless. Perhaps they married in the first place because each was lonely and desperately needed the other to fulfill that need. Marriages where each partner is using the other for unrealistic needs can soon become deserts of loneliness. They may end up suffering side by side in unbroken silence. Or perhaps the marriage began with good mutuality and maturity, but later one of the partners falls in love with someone else or with an overdemanding career. Then the other partner will have to face the desert moment of admitting to himself or herself that he no longer means anything to the one person who means everything to him.

Widows and divorcees. Widows and widowers almost inevitably experience the desert of loneliness after the death of their spouse. The closer and more dependent on one another they have been, the more painful the loneliness. Grief is a healthy reaction to the loss of a loved one; during the period of mourning, the survivor somehow interiorizes the deceased partner and time begins to heal the wound of separation. Divorced people may go through a similar process of grieving. Sometimes the wound of divorce is deeper than that of death, if one partner must bear the loneliness of having been willfully rejected by the other. The medical consequences of loneliness have recently been studied by Dr. James Lynch, a specialist in psychosomatic medicine.[4] His research suggests that loneliness may be responsible for the higher rate of heart atacks and early deaths among divorced and widowed people. Loneliness kills, literally. The stress placed on a person's physical and psychological strength by the death or rejection of a loved one is more than many people can bear. These people perish in the desert of loneliness.

Priests and religious. By their vow of chaste love priests and religious belong to everyone. Their love is free to touch all people with the care and compassion of Christ. Many times they experience a grateful and heartfelt return of love from those they serve. Yet, because they belong to everyone, some priests and religious feel they belong to no one, and they are lonely. They yearn to belong to one person fully and exclusively. They yearn for a constant companion in their life. These priests and religious are feeling the desert loneliness of their radical and total commitment to Christ. They have been called to belong fully to him and to have him for their constant companion. The love of Christ may not satisfy them as they expected, and that is their desert experience. Eventually they may discover that the love of Christ can and does satisfy them as deeply as they could ever dream; the lonely ones who do not make this discovery may become as barren and sterile as the desert itself. There is some benefit and consolation to be had from mature friendships even with persons of the opposite sex, but these relationships are limited from the start by the demands of the priestly and religious lifestyle. A hollow center of loneliness will remain until it is filled by the mysterious presence of the risen Christ, who himself experienced all possible loneliness and rejection as he hung on the cross. In the desert of loneliness priests and religious can encounter a figure raised on a cross who seems to draw them to himself. Those who yield and let themselves be drawn will learn the secret of guiding others through the pathless desert of loneliness.

Lonely institutions. Prisons, hospitals, convalescent homes, mental institutions and other places where people are shut in and unable to leave are deserts of loneliness for many of their inmates. Hospitalized people, for instance, often feel deserted. If they have no visitors they feel forgotten. If visitors come, the patient may feel the separation all the more when they leave. The sick feel cut off, stranded on their bed, while life flows by without them. If the illness is terminal, the feeling of loneliness and alienation grows even stronger for we all face death alone. The mentally ill suffer a special degree of loneliness and desertedness. I recall visiting a state hospital near Pittsburgh with three others who went regularly to sing and talk with the patients. We were admitted to a locked ward where about two dozen women lived. The two nurses who cared for them retired to their glass-enclosed office while we visited the women. These were not the most disturbed cases in the hospital, but their suffering could almost be felt in the air around them. They sat next to one another in the large room but did not speak to their neighbors. Although some were completely unresponsive to my attempts at conversation, I was able to persuade four or five to talk with me. They told of friends or family members who came to visit them and the little gifts they had brought. Later, after we had left, I was told that the patients made up these stories about frequent visitors, or imagined them. Telling me they had visitors was their way of coping with loneliness and maintaining their self-image—"I'm not alone because I still have people who love me and visit me." But the reality was just the opposite. These were desperately lonely people whose pain was, perhaps mercifully, being controlled by sedation. They are the lost ones in the desert of loneliness.

Reflection

This list of examples could have been prolonged. The Lonely Hearts Club has more members than it knows what to do with. Most of the members are unknown, anonymous. Society does not recognize loneliness as a respectable disease like cancer or coronary problems.[5] People hide their loneliness out of shame. They try not to think about it for fear it will get worse.

If we permit ourselves to think about loneliness it is possible to learn some important things about the desert experience. First of all, we can say that a certain degree of loneliness seems to be part of the human lot. There are situations and areas of life where each of us stands alone. I stand alone, as an individual human being, whenever I exert my will to make a free decision in a major matter. I alone am responsible for my free actions. When it comes to taking the blame or receiving praise for my deliberate actions and for the general direction of my life, I stand alone. No one escapes the loneliness of personal responsibility. There are other things which I must also do alone because I am an individual human being. I must die alone. No one can take my place and do my dying for me, or do my choosing, or my refusing, or my loving, or my trusting for me. Whether I like it or not I must do these things myself, in the loneliness of freedom. Sometimes I might prefer not to face my deep inner aloneness because it makes me seem so small and vulnerable, so limited and lost, so lonely. But this dimension of loneliness seems to be a permanent, built-in feature of being human.

Loneliness tells me something else about my humanness. It speaks of the basic poverty of my being. I feel lonely because I need others. I am not the All. I need to be completed by others. Loneliness is my human spirit within me longing for perfect fulfillment and vaguely sensing that this fulfillment can come only through relationships with others. People need people. I need to be close to others, work and play and communicate with them, love them and be loved by them. I am made for relationships and can never be complete without them. Loneliness is my longing for perfect relational intimacy. The feeling of lacking that intimacy is the desert experience.

The desert may drive me to seek satisfaction in pseudo-intimacy. Pseudo-intimacy offers a semblance of true affection but can never fully satisfy my loneliness. Promiscuous sex provides some people with pseudo-intimacy. The devoted attentions of a pet may provide a pseudo-intimacy for others; they soothe their loneliness with a friendly dog or cat, or a bowl of guppies. Still others may seek refuge from loneliness in the world of fantasy; they curl up with a book and withdraw to the pseudo-intimacy of imaginary people in a Gothic romance. Similarly, TV soap-operas can furnish the lonely housewife with the same soothing anodyne every afternoon.

I do not choose to be lonely, but when I am feeling lonely I do have a tendency to prolong the mood by brooding over my unhappiness and indulging in self-pity. Self-pity intensifies my loneliness, pleasantly. "I feel so alone.

Nobody understands. Nobody really cares. Nobody knows me as I want to be known." I may still have many acquaintances and friends but the affection and affirmation they supply is not enough. I feel myself being slowly squeezed into a corner where I sit alone, with the whole world against me. I eat my lonely heart out in self-pity, and rather enjoy the sensation.

Instead, with a little will-power and creative imagination, I might be able to snap out of my mood of loneliness, make new friends, discover new interests, and so on. If I stopped leaning on others I might become more self-reliant and less lonely. If I stopped thinking about myself and tried to do something for others, I might be far less lonely. I begin to move through the desert of loneliness when I stop putting myself first and expecting the world, and God, to make life comfortable for me. Life is often abrasive, like desert sand. My experience of loneliness is part of the inevitable roughness of life.

There is still another dimension of loneliness. Some people know that they are lonely for God. This loneliness is one of the hardest to bear—a desert experience in the strict sense. There is a private dimension in every human person reserved for God alone, a dimension where we remain virginal for God. When God chooses not to enter our conscious life we feel the desert experience of loneliness in a most distressing way. It may seem that he is angry with us and punishing us by withholding his favors. We might feel that God has gone off to give his lights and consolations to the professional contemplatives, leaving us neglected and lonely in the desert. We can easily fall into self-pity. The desert experience tests the fiber of our spiritual life and raises questions about our basic notion of God. Even in the desert of loneliness God remains our father, who loves us and wishes to prepare us in the desert for an intimacy we cannot imagine. As we will see in Part II, the absent God is mysteriously present in our desert experience, guiding our steps toward his land of promise, our true homeland.

Conclusion

Everything we have seen about the desert of loneliness permits the conclusion that the lonely person does not feel at home where he is. He feels he is in a strange place where he does not belong. It is desert where he is, and the desert was not meant to be his homeland. He is out of place, a stranger, a foreigner on alien soil.

The lonely feel isolated and cut off from the place where they would like to be, where they belong, where they are known, accepted, and appreciated, the place where they are secure and at home. The lonely have no home to come home to. It has been said that home is not a place but a person. Lonely people may travel far and wide looking for the person who can make them feel at home. They are searching for an oasis in the desert, a place of rich and nourishing soil where they can sink their roots and build their home.

Their search is futile. The oasis is a mirage. The desert of loneliness cannot be crossed by running away from the situation where God has placed us. The desert can be crossed only when God himself leads us across. At the deepest level of our loneliness we are lonely for God to come to us and lead us into his oasis of intimacy and rest. Until that time of rest our hearts will continue to be restless and lonely, and we will continue to be exiles and strangers in a desertland.

The greatest mistake might be to take the desertland for

our homeland and to settle for a partial satisfaction of our loneliness. The desert of loneliness is a painful but helpful reminder of our fundamental human condition as strangers and exiles. The desert is there, inside us, to challenge our sense of belonging entirely to any place or any human person. We can belong to a place and a person but not entirely. We can put down roots but not permanently, because the desert within reminds us that this is not our permanent place. Simone Weil, a young French philosopher who died in loneliness and exile, spoke from the highest perspective as well as from her personal experience when she said: "We must be rooted in the absence of a place."[6] Our actual concrete situation is where we must be rooted even in our loneliness. But the place where we concretely are is not our true and final place. It is the absence of that place. It is a desert.

CHAPTER THREE

THE DESERT OF SENSELESSNESS

The desert we will explore in this chapter is marked by the feeling both of inner emptiness and of desertedness. In this desert nothing makes much sense any more. We can see no meaning behind what is happening in our life. Life used to be worth living, but now what's the use?

A sudden tragedy in life may throw us into the desert of senselessness: a car accident claims the life of a spouse; a robbery reduces a family to poverty; a fire destroys a person's life work; a mother gives birth to a deformed child; a religious superior withdraws consent from a subject's special apostolate; a trusted friend is discovered in betrayal. The anguished question "Why? Why did this have to happen?" is wrenched from our heart and goes unanswered. The story of Job in the Old Testament is the story of a man swept into the desert of senselessness by sudden tragedy. On the same day Job lost all his possessions and all his children. Then he was afflicted with a loathsome disease. Certain of his innocence and unable to understand his misfortune, Job cursed the day of his birth and wished for death.

The crisis of meaninglessness may come less suddenly. Someone feels his life gradually slipping out of his control. His well-ordered existence is breaking up, disintegrating little by little. He questions the value of trying to keep it all together any longer. What is it all for? What is the meaning of this constant hassle? His questioning slowly undermines the foundation of the kind of life he has been living. He no longer believes in what he is doing. Eventually he will no longer believe in anything. He feels trapped in absurdity. The future looks as bleak and senseless as a desert. What is there left to live for?

Whether suddenly or slowly, the desert of senselessness empties life of its meaning and makes death seem an appealing alternative. People have the will to live only as long as they can see something worth living for—a person, a religious or political principle, a mission or duty to accomplish. When these ultimate values are called into question and lose their force of appeal, as happens in the desert experience of senselessness, then living becomes meaningless. To go on is only to prolong and compound the chaos. The human person lives by meaning. When nothing makes sense any more, he has nothing to live for.

There is no such thing as meaning in the abstract. Meaning is always found, or not found, in the actual situation and circumstances of life at a particular moment. If this situation does not make sense to me, I cannot pull meaning out of the air and make it apply. The meaning of the situation has to emerge from the situation itself. If someone else sees meaning there, perhaps he can help me make sense of it. This book, for instance, is a progressive effort on my part to share with others the meaning I believe is hidden in the desert experience.

If I listen to another's explanation of the meaning of my situation and it still does not make sense to me, I may choose to trust his vision and believe in his reading of the matter. I take it on faith. Some people can make sense of their desert experience because of their faith in God, who sees a meaning and value in everything he permits to happen. For other people the desert of senselessness obscures both their faith in life and their faith in God.

Making Sense

Imagine someone looking at the exhibits in the section of an art gallery that features contemporary paintings. He may walk past half a dozen works, shaking his head in amazement or amusement. He can make no sense of them at all. Then he comes to one that strikes him differently. He pauses before it. He may say, "I like that. I wonder what it's supposed to be." He looks at the title marker for some clue: "Number 23." With a smile and a shrug of resignation he walks on.

What can we say about the pictures that man saw? The first ones were meaningless to him. Number 23 spoke to him and seemed to make sense in some obscure way, even though he could not say exactly what it meant. When something makes sense to me it makes an appeal to my reason and feeling and sense of value; it lights up for me, becomes alive for me, stands out among other things and engages me in some vital way. Meaning makes life worth living. In the desert experience the springs of living meaning have dried up for me, leaving a dry wasteland. Nothing any longer lights up for me and engages me vitally. Again and again I ask, "Why?" but no answer echoes back from the faceless desert. Senselessness on all sides.

How do I make sense? Since I am not born with a built-in set of meanings, I must discover for myself what makes sense. All my life I am in search of meanings to live by. I need a solid ground of meaning to stand on and a network of meaningful human relationships to move about in. I journey through life with sensitive antennas ready to turn toward the objects that resonate most deeply for me, the objects that speak to my heart. From these objects—assorted values and goals—and from my field of human relationships I piece together the meaning of life. I try to make sense of my life. In the desert experience the fabric of meaning I have so carefully woven begins to come apart of itself.

The institutions and structures of our society exist to hold together a meaningful, orderly life for the majority of citizens. Society defines what is meaningful and communicates these meanings so that the average citizen will be able to make sense out of his life even when disordered conditions prevail around him.[1] By subscribing to everything society proposes, I might possibly be spared some of the desert of senselessness. If I wish to live by its judgments society has explanations for everything I could question in life. When I do not know what to do, society through advertising techniques suggests personal goals and consumer goods to strive for. The law tells me how to behave and how not to behave and has sanctions for those individuals whose personal style does not conform to the common standards of the culture. My functioning in daily life is regulated by social customs that tell me where to go, what to say and do, when to begin and finish, and what attitude to have throughout. My interpersonal relationships as a social being are in part governed by an accepted class system based on such criteria as wealth, power, and race. My aesthetic response to the horizon of beauty and value in life is largely limited to the objects proposed to me by the mass communications media. In all these ways society mediates to me its own sense, its own understanding of what life is all about.

In their compulsion to make sense out of every aspect of their life, some people go to the extreme of trying to be in total control of their little corner of the world. They organize and plan to the last possible detail. By trying to bring rational order to every situation they impose their own meanings before the intrinsic order and meaning can emerge from deep within the situation itself. They try to have everything in life on their own terms, try to engineer their own security, try to assure their own comfortable future. Unfortunately, their very fear of losing control may lead them into the desert of senselessness. Too much organizing, too much having and consuming, too many needs and desires may empty life of its power to entice and to satisfy. In the end such people wander hopelessly in the desert of their own planned, calculated and controlled existence.

The thirst for total sense and clarity is a desert mirage. A realistic outlook on life is satisfied with making partial sense. If I see *some* meaning in the events and direction of my life, that may be all I can realistically expect. Reality, even the limited reality of my own life, is too vast to manage and manipulate. I cannot see the future. And the past is a tangled web of contingencies, any one of which might have changed the course of my life. My present situation lies at the end of a long road of "ifs"—If I had done or said this instead of that, if I had gone there instead of here, if only I had known. . . . But who can know and foresee and plan for everything, or understand why things were meant to be this way? We can try to understand, but we may have to be content with making only partial sense out of the situation. For the rest, we stand in the desert of senselessness along with a large number of other people.

The desert seems to resist stubbornly my attempts to make sense of it. The desert refuses to cooperate with my carefully made plans, time-tables, and projects for my life. I have to face the fact that I no longer have everything under control. In the desert experience of senselessness I face the recalcitrance of reality, and even the apparent maliciousness of reality. The things that matter most in my life, and the people that matter most, are beyond my power to manipulate and direct the way I wish. In the desert experience I make the discovery that things and persons are as they are, and not necessarily as I thought they would be or tried to make them be. And life is as it is even though I cannot see why it should be this way.

The question raised by the desert of senselessness is whether or not I can live with things the way they are. Can I *accept* what I am and where I am, and try to function within these given limits, or will I go on trying to tame the unconquerable desert? Acceptance does not mean inert, fatalistic passivity, or anesthetized insensitivity, or a rigid, grit-your-teeth stoicism in the face of absurdity and injustice. Acceptance lies along the path of courageous, patient endurance of things I cannot understand or change. Acceptance is the opposite of a calculating, ego-powered effort to organize and make sense of everything by subjecting it to my control. If I can accept the desert experience I let go of the reins of overcontrol, let things unfold according to their own inner truth, and remain genuinely open to all the meanings and potentialities that may be present in my situation.

If I try to fight the desert I may be destined to wither and die in the desert, but if I can somehow accept my desert experience in the full horizon of my human potential and my faith, I may find myself transformed by the experience. I may slowly be purified, seasoned, liberated, matured. Life can seem far more precious for being demanding. Experiences that draw out the best that is in us help us attain the full stature of selfhood.

In the desert of arid emptiness and meaninglessness the

issue that ultimately faces me is life or death. If I accept my desert experience, I make an option for life and choose life no matter what life may bring to me. Such a response calls for all the courage I can summon. It takes courage simply to be, to go on living when there is nothing left to live for. Theologian and philosopher Paul Tillich writes about the courageous and grateful acceptance of the mystery of life in spite of the life-denying forces of the desert. He affirms: "The act of accepting meaninglessness is in itself a meaningful act."[2] That act of accepting is courage. Tillich's notion of courage is not the kind of courage we might associate with a soldier moving into combat with the enemy. Courage in Tillich's sense is not active resistance but active acceptance. In an intrinsically meaningful act, courage takes in the desert experience, takes it upon itself, embraces it, and in that very embrace affirms life, being, and meaning in spite of the desert. Courageous acceptance transforms senselessness into *some* sense at least. My act of acceptance is a meaningful act that elevates me above my desert experience and inserts me more deeply into the mystery of life. In acceptance, life triumphs over the lifeless desert.

The Plague

We have been theorizing about the desert of senselessness and possible responses to this desert experience. It is time now to check our theory against the facts of life. Is it possible to practice courageous acceptance of senselessness when, for instance, my doctor tells me that he has found advanced cancer and I have only about four months to live? Or when my closest friend has an accident diving in a shallow lake and is left a paraplegic with one per cent functioning from the neck down? Or when I have an alcoholic spouse, or a severely retarded son? These are desert experiences of senselessness. In the life of a priest or religious this desert may come when he or she meets with a disenchanting failure and concludes that the consecrated life is not what the vocation brochures pictured it to be. The ideal of selfless love and apostolic zeal becomes a cruel illusion when success and prestige seem to be the name of the game in my community. Is there any use in being a priest or religious any longer? Would such a life be useful to anyone?

To study any one of these possible and actual desert experiences of people today might restrict the experience unnecessarily. Instead I am going to reflect on a literary experience that may be more universal and easier to identify with in its essential elements. Great works of literature are paradigms of universal human experience. The work we will consider is *The Plague* by Albert Camus, spokesman for the senselessness and absurdity of human existence.[3]

The principal characters in *The Plague,* Dr. Bernard Rieux and Fr. Paneloux, are studies in alternative responses to the presence of evil and absurdity in the world. The bubonic plague that descended on the city of Oran, Algeria, and sealed it off from the rest of the world for twelve months, was Camus' symbol for all that is evil in the world and in man. The plague moved in, ran its course, then moved on again until the next time, like the movement of some inexorable fate which man could struggle against if he wished, or could endure if he could, but which might not be overcome. There was no medical cure or antidote available.

Dr. Bernard Rieux is presented as a man of great sensitivity, sympathy, and compassion. The plague has separated him from his wife who is in a sanatorium a hundred miles away. In the early stages of the plague Rieux's task was to travel through the city, identify cases of the plague, and have them committed to hospitals where they would eventually die. The doctor's best friend, Tarrou, asks him at one point, "Do you believe in God, doctor?" After reflecting briefly Rieux replies, "No—but what does that really mean? I'm fumbling in the dark, struggling to make something out" [p. 116]. Tarrou asks how he can show so much devotion to the sick if he has no faith in God. The author puts the reply in the third person:

> His face still in shadow, Rieux said that he's already answered: that if he believed in an all-powerful God he would cease curing the sick and leave that to Him. But no one in the world believed in a God of that sort; no, not even Paneloux, who believed that he believed in such a God. And this was proved by the fact that no one ever threw himself on Providence completely. Anyhow, in this respect Rieux believed himself to be on the right road—in fighting against creation as he found it [p. 116].

What Rieux is really fighting against is death. Rieux loves life and loves people; he has never gotten used to seeing people suffer and die. How could there be a God who sits silently by while people suffer and die? Rieux says to Tarrou: "Since the order of the world is shaped by death, mightn't it be better for God if we refuse to believe in Him, and struggle with all our might against death, without raising our eyes towards the heaven where He sits in silence?" [p. 117]. Rieux could never bring himself to believe in or to love such a God: "Until my dying day I shall refuse to love a scheme of things in which children are put to torture" [p. 197].

Rieux has chosen for himself the role of healer, trying to bring peace to those in pain. He realized that his victories would never be lasting; in reality he faces a never ending defeat. But that is his path, his job, his destiny. He is not trying to be a hero or a saint but simply a man, one who struggles even as he is defeated [see p. 231]. It is a great blow for Rieux when Tarrou dies of the plague and he can do nothing but stand impotently by as his friend agonizes. The next morning there is a final blow when Rieux receives word of his wife's death also. Outwardly he retained his composure; inwardly he agonized.

As a memorial of the injustice and outrage done to himself and to his fellow citizens by the plague, Rieux wrote a chronicle of those months. There he recorded what had been done by men in their never ending fight against terror, done by men who, "unable to be saints but refusing to bow down to pestilences, strive their utmost to be healers" [p. 278]. Rieux's conclusion is that "there are more things to admire in men than to despise" [p. 278].

Dr. Rieux tried to make sense of the desert in plague-stricken Oran by doing something about it, rather than by sitting back and philosophizing about it. Father Paneloux, the other main protagonist, tried to make sense first of all by reasoning and by appealing to the authority of scripture. Paneloux's efforts, as reported in the first of two sermons that he gave, were unconvincing. The theme of the first sermon was that the plague came from God as punishment for the sins of the people of Oran. Paneloux was speaking from the outside, as one not personally involved in the fault or the punishment.

Later Paneloux decided to join Rieux's band of paramedics to work in the hospitals among the dying. There he was obliged to watch an innocent child die in agony after an experimental injection had failed to help him. That event changed Paneloux's response to the desert of senselessness. The tormented death of the innocent youngster placed Paneloux solidly and personally in the desert.

Then he preached his second sermon. Instead of saying "You" to his congregation, he now said "We." He had identified himself with their plight. In this sermon Paneloux squarely confronted the desert mystery of the suffering of the innocent, a mystery whose senselessness raised gigantic questions for this priest's faith in God. Paneloux felt he was at a moment of testing and crisis. He said to the congregation:

> My brothers, a time of testing has come for us all. We must believe everything or deny everything. And who, I ask, amongst you would dare to deny everything? . . . Religion in a time of plague could not be the religion of every day. . . . Today God has vouchsafed to His creatures an ordeal such that they must acquire and practice the greatest of all virtues: that of the All or Nothing [202].

Paneloux presented his congregation with a difficult option: to accept everything in the name of faith or to deny everything. He offered no way out of the dilemma, nothing to soothe the painful choice he saw. He explicitly faced the mystery of innocent suffering:

> We must hold fast, trusting in the divine goodness, even as to the deaths of little children, and not seeking personal respite. . . . We must convince ourselves that there is no island of escape in time of plague. No, there was no middle course. We must accept the dilemma: and choose either to

hate God or to love God. And who would dare to choose to hate Him? My brothers—the preacher's tone showed he was nearing the conclusion of his sermon—the love of God is a hard love. It demands total self-surrender, disdain of our human personality. And yet it alone can reconcile us to suffering and the deaths of children, it alone can justify them, since we cannot understand them, and we can only make God's will ours [p. 205].

Fr. Paneloux was exhorting himself as much as his congregation, for he did not find it easy to surrender in the desert when he could not understand. Yet somehow he found the courage to practice the harsh doctrine he was preaching. A few days after the sermon Paneloux came down with the fever. He submitted passively to Dr. Rieux's ministrations, without permitting himself to hope for a cure. He was willing to suffer and be destroyed, holding fast to a "hard love" of God, to a divine will he could not understand. He kept faith even when faith seemed folly.

Reflection

Both Dr. Rieux and Fr. Paneloux were caught in the desert of senselessness, and each had a different response. The author, Camus, stresses the intransigence of both characters, Rieux with his heroic refusal to give up the struggle against death and Paneloux with his total self-surrender to the incomprehensible goodness of God. But Paneloux is painted as a religious fanatic, a fool who deserves to be laughed at. It is Rieux who has the author's complete sympathy as a model of human dignity and courage in the desert of an absurd existence.

When we reflect more closely on Rieux's response, which seems so courageous and creditable at first sight, the doctor appears as the symbol of rebellion, revolt, and retaliation against the desert. Rieux, the noble and dignified humanitarian, will conquer the desert and bring sense into the senseless universe by his own unaided power. For Rieux has refused to appeal for help to any power other than human calculation and inventiveness. God seems to have sent the plague to Oran; Rieux will not appeal to God to take it away. God has been judged and condemned for not measuring up to human standards, Rieux's standards.

Rieux chose to become a healer, that is a savior, almost in defiance of a God who apparently "sits in silence" in heaven. A God who can remain aloof from human misery is more politely ignored than spoken of. Rieux could not bring himself to address such a God with a plea for mercy and salvation. The only hope he saw for salvation was in human teamwork, the progress of medical science and technology, and all the other aspects of man's courageous struggle against the defective and dangerous world he lives in. Rieux was dedicated to "fighting against creation as he found it." Even so, he knew he could not hope to exercise more than a temporary holding action against the forces of absurdity and evil. Ultimately he too would die and be absorbed into the meaningless, indifferent, insensitive universe that surrounded him.

In fairness to Rieux it must be said that the questions he faced are far from simple. He faced a mystery of senselessness concentrated to a point of maddening intensity in the city of Oran. The suffering of the innocent is a sad and scandalous fact. The world we live in is far from perfect. But Rieux's response is not the most creative and humanizing solution. Revolt and rebellion may be heroic but they attack the problem on its own ground. These options pertain to the mode of domination, control, manipulation, mastery. When order and meaning are not given, or are not immediately evident in the situation, our first reaction is often to reach out and forcefully impose order on chaos. By our own authority and the resources of our own human spirit we forge our own life meanings, values, goals.

Once Dr. Rieux had decided to revolt against the way things were, and against the God who permitted them to be that way, he was obliged to create health and happiness in Oran by his own power. He proceeded to impose on others and on the situation his own vision of the way things should be done. Declining to believe in God, Rieux elevated himself to the throne of healer and savior in an attempt to be his own God.

If we turn to Fr. Paneloux we see a man who does not surrender his faith in God, but whose idea of God is sadly warped—a God who manifests his goodness and takes his delight in the suffering of innocent children. To this concept of God Paneloux is uncompromisingly loyal, to the point of extremism and absolutism. Paneloux's well-meant but misguided rigidity is never softened by the recollection of God's hidden presence in the innocent, senselessly suffering Christ on the cross. In the response Paneloux makes to his desert experience of senselessness we miss a flowing flexibility and a gentle capability to roll with the punches of life. He sees life too much as either-or: either all black or all white, either all senseless or all meaningful, either All or Nothing. Neither Fr. Paneloux nor Dr. Rieux offers us a perfect model of a courageous and liberating response to the desert of senselessness.

Acceptance in Faith

In the desert of senselessness I can no longer see my way through the chaos and confusion in which I live. I am lost, wandering in a vicious circle on the surface of an endless desert. I am unable to go anywhere; my journey through life has become a going around in circles, as senseless as a dog chasing his tail. I feel tied to a revolving wheel, going around and around and getting nowhere. Perhaps my fate is to be like the Israelites who spent forty years wandering aimlessly in the desert, under sentence of slow death for their disbelief. The whole generation that left Egypt behind God's mighty hand and outstretched arm perished in the wilderness. Perhaps there are certain situations in life, like the desert experience, that cannot be conquered and mastered, and the best alternative is to accept them, make partial sense of them if possible, and let them work themselves out in my living through them or my dying in them. The courage to live and to die is given to me when I accept the desert of senselessness with faith in the mystery of life. Acceptance in faith means going along with life without despair and without revolt, trusting that all things are guided by the mysterious, unseen hand of God, including such things as the vicious circle of meaninglessness disorder, and death. Theologian Jürgen Moltmann speaks of acceptance in Christian faith when he promises: "In the vicious circle of meaninglessness and godforsakenness, finally, [God] comes forward in the figure of the crucified Christ, who communicates courage to be."[4]

Acceptance in faith does not mean I will be able to *see* God in a cloud by day and a pillar of fire by night leading me through the desert. Faith does not see God; it surrenders to the mystery of God. Faith does not explain the apparent absence of God in the desert experience, it accepts the absence. Faith does not attempt to interpret or justify what God permits to happen in the world; instead it patiently sustains everything. The more impenetrable and incomprehensible the mystery, the deeper is the faith that is called forth. In the desert experience of senselessness, God is absent. Yet I can accept in faith the mystery of his absence and can surrender to him from the depths of my emptiness and desertedness.

Conclusion

We have been investigating a desert region that has been drained dry of all meaning, all human purpose in living. I have stressed, perhaps over-stressed, the *exterior* events and situations that may turn my life into a desert of senselessness. But the desert is within me as much as it is outside. By my interior attitude, of rebellion or of acceptance in faith, I can modify that desert outside. It is a mistake to concentrate on transforming the exterior desert situation and neglect the desert within. I think T.S. Eliot sounded an appropriate warning when he wrote:

Second, you neglect and belittle the desert.
The desert is not remote in southern tropics,
The desert is not only around the corner,
The desert is squeezed in the tube-train next to you,
The desert is in the heart of your brother.[5]

Eliot sees that the desert is not merely that geographical area of wasteland in the southern tropics, nor that meaningless and absurd situation that may be facing me around the corner. The desert is a dryness and loneliness and emptiness found much closer to home. The desert is in the heart of my brother on the subway and in my own heart too. The desert experience of senselessness leaves a cavity, an inner void, within me where nothing lights up or calls to me or comes alive. The emptiness I feel is a spiritual vacuum, like the physical vacuum of outer space. In the inner space of my heart there is not an atom of meaningfulness, but only a devouring emptiness that draws everything into its own absurdity. I cry out, "Why? For what purpose?" There is no reply; my questions are lost in the silent vastness of the desert. In this chapter we have seen that the greatest degree of peace and potential growth lies in a faith-acceptance of not having the answers or the clarity I long for. We have not yet seen why acceptance should bring peace in the desert, and the reason will not be evident until we place the desert experience more explicitly in the context of Christian revelation and the history of salvation. The deepest meaning of the desert experience will be clarified as we reflect in Part II on the rich heritage of spirituality in the Judaeo-Christian tradition.

PART II

DESERT EXPERIENCE IN THE CONTEXT OF SALVATION HISTORY

INTRODUCTION

Because I am a Christian who has had a long exposure to the teachings contained in the sacred scripture and doctrine of my religion, I tend to interpret the desert experience in the light of what Christian revelation has to say about desertedness and emptiness. Were I a Buddhist, I would probably interpret the desert experience in the context of the Buddhist doctrine of *Sunyata*—emptiness, the void. Each person understands and articulates his lived experience in the conceptual framework most accessible to him.

As a Christian I believe that the Father has sent his only Son to save mankind and draw all people into divine nearness, love, and sonship, through the power of his Holy Spirit. But in my desert experience I no longer feel God's loving presence. I feel the absence of divine nearness, love, and Fatherly care. How can I, as long as I am in the desert, go on trusting and believing in this absent God?

In Part II, I will answer this question in the terms most accessible to me as Christian, namely the terms of explicit public revelation in the Old and New Testament. Scripture is the story of the dealings between God and humanity from the creation of the world to the new creation accomplished by Jesus Christ. The desert is a theme of major importance in the Old Testament and in the life of Jesus himself.

The Old and the New Testament are the context in which I will examine contemporary desert experience. In Chapter Four we will listen to the story of the desert experience as it resonates in Judaeo-Christian tradition. In Chapter Five we will relate some aspects of the contemporary desert experience, especially in the life of prayer, to the scriptural context.

In the desert experience, when we have given up hope we have given up everything. Yet the desert stretches our hope to the breaking point. The desert experience takes the measure of our living trust in God, in life, and in ourselves. In Part II the theme of trust will recur like a refrain. Seen in the context of salvation history, the desert experience seems designed to strengthen our trust, so that we learn to hope even in a hopeless situation. When we can no longer trust and rely on our own ability to make sense of the situation and bring things under our control, we learn the lesson of trusting in the constant care and guidance of God. God is leading those who trust his promises to the far side of the desert. Salvation history assures us that the desert does not last forever. Endless though the desert may seem when we are in it, a spirit of trust never doubts that we are on the way to a rich land. Trust tends to transform the way into the goal itself and change the desert into streams of clear water. This prospect is part of the faith-vision we see preserved in the pages of the Old and New Testament.

CHAPTER FOUR

DESERT EXPERIENCE IN SCRIPTURE

When I am going through a desert experience in my life, I want to know what is going on in this situation. The situation will remain objectively the same, but my way of looking at it may make the difference between growth in the desert and death in the desert. I can perceive my desert experience as a mysterious pathway to the promised land, or I can perceive it as a wasteland of desertedness and emptiness where I am completely and permanently lost. I can perceive my desert experience as a period of psychological depression that I can correct by taking the proper pill, or I can perceive it as a period of spiritual testing and purification sent by God to lead me towards deeper freedom and wholeness.

How am I to discern what is truly going on? Consultation with a competent spiritual director would be helpful, but is not always possible. The question that eventually has to be faced, whether alone or with a helper, is this: In my desert experience of God's absence is God somehow still lovingly present and watchful or not? Judged merely intellectually there are usually enough reasons for doubting God's presence and action as for believing it. The way I choose to read the situation will depend not only on intellectual judgment but on my general life orientation—my "spirit" or "heart" as scripture calls it [see Nm 14:24].

In the present chapter I am suggesting that the right spirit in which to look at the desert experience is to see it as a personal participation in salvation history. Throughout history God is continually leading his people out of bondage in Egypt, through the desert, to the spiritual maturity and freedom of a transformed existence. Jesus himself went through the desert of dereliction on the cross to rise in the glory of his paschal life. The desert experience of the Israelites in the Old Testament and the desert experience of Jesus are situations that tell us about God's favored modes of interacting with his people. Such situations are called "key situations" by Adrian van Kaam, leading exponent of formative spirituality.

Key Situations[1]

Van Kaam observes that we are inserted inescapably into human history in ways that permeate and affect our most basic experience of ourselves. Paying attention to these historical influences is the key to the deeper meaning of all our experiences, including the experiences of the spiritual life. God can speak to us and act in our life through influential key situations. Three of the key situations described by van Kaam are important for us to consider here.

Historical Christian key situations are the situations and events through which God revealed himself to the people of Israel, to the primitive Christian community, and continues to reveal himself to the church down through the centuries. The written record of these historical key situations is to be found in the Old and New Testament, in the teachings of the church, and in the writings of the saints. Historical key situations are co-extensive with the whole of salvation history.

Personal key situations are the fundamental circumstances and events that constitute a person's own life history. Family, race, religion, economic status, country and community, educational opportunities, cultural influences, environmental factors, political events—all these determine a person's life history and constitute his personal key situations. Personal key situations affect a person both consciously and preconsciously, depending on how aware of them he may be.

Daily life situations are also key situations. A person's actual or current key situation is made up of the things he faces here and now in his daily life. The daily key situation provides the objects—persons, events, things—with which a person interacts. People live and act within the context of their actual, everyday, key situations.

These three exterior key situations penetrate the Christian, become interior to him, become part of him, and modify him from within. Let us reflect on these ideas to see how they apply to desert experience.

Reflection

My personal key situation includes my daily life situation, and these intertwine with all the historical Christian key situations. I am not living through my desert experience in total historical isolation, as if I were the only person ever to have experienced the desert in my spiritual life. The key situation of my daily life may be a desert experience of dryness as I attempt to spend half an hour in meditation, but that key situation hooks into my personal key situation and into the larger historical Christian key situation as well. My current desert experience is permeated and modified by the other key situations that I have absorbed simply by the fact of being part of the stream of history. As a Christian I am part of the history of salvation and of revelation.

In my current situation of desertedness and emptiness, God seems painfully absent from my life. Yet I believe that God can be present and speaking to me through other key situations of my life. In order to listen to God's word to me I must tune in to my historical and personal key situations. By an attentive reading of these situations I can come to know what is going on in my current desert experience situation. In this chapter we will be paying special attention to the historical desert experiences of the Old and New Testament which are key situations for my own desert experience as a Christian.

The desert experience of the contemporary Christian is best understood in the light of Jesus' own desert experience. But since Jesus himself was situated in the history of his people, his desert experience can best be understood in the light of the exodus of the Israelites out of Egypt into the desert. Part A of this chapter will be devoted to the Old Testament desert experience and Part B to the New Testament desert experience.

PART A

DESERT EXPERIENCE IN THE OLD TESTAMENT

The desert experience of the people of God is an historical key situation and one of the archetypal themes of the Old Testament. The experience occurred during the forty year period that the Israelites wandered aimlessly through the deserts of the Sinai peninsula, the period between the miraculous crossing of the Red Sea and the crossing of the Jordan River into the land of Canaan that God had promised to give them. Israel remembered the experience with both shame and nostalgia. The desert exposed the disobedience, petulance and headstrong character of the people; God punished them by permitting an entire generation to die there. But the desert was also remembered as the time when they lacked nothing, a time of privileged nearness to God when he was in their midst leading them with infinite tenderness and care. We will listen as the scriptures again tell their intricate story.

The Story of the Desert

In Egypt the people of God were groaning under the yoke of slavery and oppression. God heard their cry, saw their plight, and resolved "to rescue them from the Egyptians and bring them up out of that land to a land fine and large, to a land flowing with milk and honey" [Ex 3:7-8]. Only after a long series of plagues did Pharaoh permit the Hebrews to leave the country, with all their possessions, for the purpose of offering sacrifices to God in the desert. So the people of God made their exodus, passing through the Red Sea on dry ground, "the water forming a wall for them to right and left of them" [Ex 14:29]. When the waters closed behind them, their pursuers were cut off from following, and the Hebrews were cut off from returning. They found themselves in a pathless desert, far away from the promised land.

God himself led his people through the desert, going before them in the form of a cloud, traveling by slow and easy stages. "It was at the bidding of the Lord that the Israelites set out, and it was at the bidding of the Lord that they camped" [Nm: 9:18]. Their immediate destination was Mount Sinai (also called Horeb). To reach Sinai they had to pass through the desert of Shur or Etham, and the desert of Sin. At each stage of the journey the "whole Israelite community grumbled against Moses and Aaron in the desert" because they did not have sufficient water to drink or flesh to eat [Ex 16:21]. Then God supplied them with sweet water, with quail, and with manna, until they came to Sinai. There Moses received the commandments from God; at the very same time the people who were camped in the desert at the foot of the mountain built a golden calf and worshipped it.

From Sinai the cloud led the people to the desert of Paran where they again complained about the lack of flesh to eat. An advance scouting party gave the community a bad report about the land of promise, so that nearly the whole community was in favor of going back. " 'Let us take our own course and return to Egypt,' they said to one another" [Nm 14:4]. At that, God's anger blazed against his people and he said:

> Of all the men who have seen my glory and the signs I worked in Egypt and in the desert, and who nevertheless

have put me to the test ten times already and have failed to heed my voice, not one shall see the land which I promised on oath to their fathers. . . . Here in the desert they shall die to the last man [Nm 14:22-23, 35].

For forty years God led the community around in circles in the desert until the first generation died off. He provided them with water, manna, and quail, but he would not let them enter the promised land until he had taught them their lesson. Moses and Aaron offended God at the waters of Kadesh Maribah, in the desert of Zin, and they forfeited their right to enter the promised land although they were permitted to view it from a distance:

Because you were not faithful to me in showing forth my sanctity before the Israelites, you shall not lead this community into the land I will give them [Nm 20:12].

Despite the lack of trust and the ingratitude of the first generation, God's plan eventually prevailed, and misfortune was turned to rejoicing as the second-generation Israelites entered the promised land under the leadership of Joshua and Kaleb. These were God's chosen people, who had come to know him during their long desert experience:

I led you for forty years in the desert. Your clothes did not fall from you in tatters nor your sandals from your feet; bread was not your food, nor wine or beer your drink. Thus you should know that I, the Lord, am your God [Dt 29:4-5].

God warned his people not to forget their desert experience:

> Be careful not to forget the Lord, your God . . . who
> brought you out of the land of Egypt, that place of slavery;
> who guided you through the vast and terrible desert with
> its saraph serpents and scorpions, its parched and waterless
> ground; who brought forth water for you from the flinty
> rock and fed you in the desert with manna, a food
> unknown to your fathers, that he might afflict you and test
> you, but also make you prosperous in the end [Dt 8:11-16].

We can summarize the desert experience of the people of
God by saying that in general it was a period in which God
tested his people, instructed them, chastised them, and
purified them for the promised land. Time and again they
were unfaithful to him but eventually they came to know
that he was their God and they were his people. It was in
the desert that they entered into a covenant with God and
received the revelation of his law. The desert experience
formed the motley bands of Hebrew refugees into a community with an identity of its own. That transformation
process went on during forty years of desert wandering.
During their desert years they learned to depend entirely on
God to feed, to lead, and to defend them. They learned to
know him by his deeds for them.

Centuries later Ezra, the scribe, looked back on the
history of his people and recalled God's wonderful works
in the desert. In his prayer Ezra praised God for being slow
to anger and abounding in mercy:

> . . . in your great mercy you did not forsake them in the
> desert. The column of cloud did not cease to lead them by
> day on their journey, nor did the column of fire by night
> cease to light for them the way by which they were to
> travel. Your good spirit you bestowed on them, to give

them understanding; your manna you did not withhold from their mouths, and you gave them water in their thirst. Forty years in the desert you sustained them: they did not want; their garments did not become worn, and their feet did not become swollen [Neh 9:19-21].

Subsequent History

Even in the promised land the Israelites were never far from the physical desert. The desert was there as a constant reminder of the desert experience their ancestors went through. They told and re-told the story of those years and kept the memory alive. In retrospect the desert experience was gradually idealized. I have selected a few examples to show how the desert retained an abiding influence on the people of God.

The Rechabites. In their desert experience the people of God were a people *en route,* a nomadic people, a pilgrim people, never settling permanently until they reached the promised land. The thirty-fifth chapter of *Jeremiah* tells us that the primitive nomadic tradition was still alive until the Babylonian captivity. The Rechabites, descendants of Rechab, were desert nomads and shepherds. They led a poor and austere life, perhaps in protest to the style of life being led in the cities. They drank no wine, owned no vineyards or fields, and did not build permanent houses but lived in tents, following their flocks from one desert pasturage to another.

Elijah.[2] The prophet Elijah had his desert experience when he fled for his life from the wrath of Queen Jezebel. He left his servant at the edge of the desert of Beersheba, "and went a day's journey into the desert until he came to a broom tree and sat beneath it" [1 Kgs 19:4]. He was all alone, thwarted by Jezebel, totally drained of the will to fight, physically and psychologically exhausted. Collapsing beside the broom tree, "he prayed for death: 'This is enough, O Lord! Take my life, for I am no better than my fathers' " [1 Kgs 19:4]. Elijah fell asleep, wishing for death. But he was awakened twice by an angel of the Lord who sustained him with water and a hearth cake, just as the Lord had nourished his people with manna and water for forty years in the desert. "Then strengthened by that food, he walked forty days and forty nights to the mountain of God, Horeb" [1 Kgs 19:8]. The text does not tell us Elijah's thoughts during that long, silent, tedious march through the desert, but he was repeating the desert experience of the people of God. As the days wore on, Elijah learned that he could endure far more than he ever expected. He let God lead him through the desert to Horeb. The sacred mountain drew him like a magnet, with its promise of safety, rest, and an intimate encounter with God. The prophet's hopes were not disappointed; once he had crossed the desert he witnessed a theophany on Horeb, received a new mission, and went off rejuvenated.

Hosea. The prophet Hosea lived when the kingdoms of Israel and Judah had committed great harlotry by turning away from God to follow the Canaanite gods, the Baals. In punishment God threatened to devastate his unfaithful spouse and make her a wilderness: "I will strip her naked, leaving her as on the day of her birth; I will make her like the desert, reduce her to an arid land, and slay her with thirst" [Hos 2:3]. It was God's plan that this chastisement would make his people return to him: "And she shall say, 'I will go back to my first husband, for it was better with me then than now' " [Hos 2:7]. Then God would take his people back. Their desert experience would be turned from a time of punishment to a time of purification and renewed intimacy with God. God himself seems to long for that intimacy with his people: "I will allure her; I will lead her into the desert and speak to her heart. . . . She shall respond there as in the days of her youth, when she came up from the land of Egypt" [Hos 2:14-15]. The desert is the place of betrothal, where Israel will again come to know her God. He will say to them, "You are my people," and they will say, "My God" [Hos 2:23]. Hosea shows God as the one who takes the initiative to lead his people into the desert, whether to chasten and purify or to speak tenderly and intimately to them.

Qumran.[3] The Essene community at Qumran was a separatist, monastic movement in continuity with the desert experience tradition of the Old Testament. The Essenes went out into the physical desert near the Dead Sea in order to study the Torah and prepare for the coming redeemer, as it is written: "In the wilderness prepare the way of the Lord, make straight in the desert a highway for our God" [Is 40:3]. At the end of the Old Testament period we still find people wanting to re-live in a literal way the desert experience of their Hebrew ancestors and ready to structure their lives as much as possible after the pattern revealed in the desert.

John the Baptist.[4] We know of John only from the New Testament, but he was the last and greatest of the Old Testament prophets [see Mt 11: 9-14]. John appeared in the desert dressed like the prophet Elijah and living the life of an ascetic. The theme of John's preaching was: "Reform your lives! The reign of God is at hand" [Mt 3:2]. Crowds came to him and John exhorted them to repent, confess their sins, and be baptized in the Jordan

River. Soon a community of disciples formed around John, but it was not John's intention to initiate a mass movement out into the physical desert. Instead he called for a moral reform of life and a return to God's favor; he called for a voluntary desert experience of purification and rededication to God. John the Baptist stood on the threshold of the messianic age; he was a prophet pointing to "one more powerful" who was to come and baptize people "in the Holy Spirit" [Mk 1:7-8]. God was about to act powerfully and definitively in human history, fashioning for himself a new people in the desert of penitence and expiation. When Jesus stepped into the Jordan to be baptized, a new and faithful Israel was crossing the parted waters of the Red Sea. "Immediately the spirit drove him out into the desert" [Mk 1:12].

Reflection

Before considering the desert experience of Jesus we need to sharpen our understanding of what the Old Testament says about desert experience. The desert is both a geographical and a symbolic reality in the history of the people of God.[5] Desert experience refers, according to the Old Testament, not only to a time and place but also to a state or condition. To say *desert* is to evoke a whole tradition, going back a thousand years to the time when God brought his people out of bondage in Egypt and forged them into a chosen community in the wasteland of the Sinai peninsula. The desert experience is an historical key situation, with implications for the lives of Christians today; that is why we have dealt at length with the Old Testament account.

What happened in the desert was the prototype of an experience that would be repeated down through salvation history as God disciplined his people, as a man disciplines his sons, in order to bring them to perfect maturity. Moses warned the people never to forget that original desert experience:

> Remember how for forty years now the Lord, your God, has directed all your journeying in the desert, so as to test you by affliction and find out whether or not it was your intention to keep his commandments [Dt 8:2].

So the memory of the desert experience was preserved through the centuries. St. Paul could go so far as to say that the desert events happened precisely in order to be a sign for later days: "The things that happened to them serve as an example; they have been written as a warning to us, upon whom the end of the ages has come" [1 Cor 10:11]. The key situation of the Old Testament is the exemplar of what happens in the desert experience of Christians today.

Through the desert. In their desert experience Christians today are living the mystery of being led by God through the desert to the promised land. A desert is a harsh and inhospitable place to be. Barrenness, the inability to sustain life, seems to be one of the desert's chief characteristics. In the open desert everyone is vulnerable, exposed, at the mercy of the wilderness. Compared to the open desert, even the slavery of Egypt looked good. The Hebrews who had lived in Egypt were always ready to go back where they came from. They were afraid to go forward; the only sensible decision, they thought, was to go back to Egypt. The younger generation, under the leadership of Joshua and Kaleb, were of a different spirit [Nm 14:24]. They did not relish the desert any more than their fathers, but they had a sense of being on a journey through the desert to a land far better than anything the slave-masters would offer them in Egypt. They trusted that God could lead his people through the desert to a land flowing with milk and honey, just as he had led them across the Red Sea and brought water from the rock and food from the sky to keep them alive in the desert. What was impossible for them was possible for the Lord of the desert who is the God of infinite possibilities. For the rebellious generation the desert brought only death, but for the generation under Joshua and Kaleb it brought a revelation of who God is and it taught them "complete and continuous dependence" on him alone.[6]

Dependence and rebellion. The survival of the Israelites was constantly threatened in the desert. As long as they placed their trust in God and not in themselves, he provided unfailing help and protection. But God's presence was an elusive and intangible matter, completely free, never under the Israelites' control. God appeared in, and was effectively hidden by, a cloud or a pillar of fire. Only with Moses did God speak face to face [Nm 12:7-8]. God's mysterious presence with his people in their desert experience transformed their hopeless situation. He is the faithful one who does not abandon his people but shares their desert journey in his own way. Those who expected more of him than they had a right to expect discovered that he was quick to accept a challenge and to punish those who put his word to the test. "Like everything in the wilderness, [Yahweh's presence] is not given in terms desired or expected," observes scripture scholar Walter Brueggemann.[7] God *was* present, but his presence was enigmatic and not to be presumed upon. He prolonged the desert experience of those who rebelled against his leadership, and after forty years the entire generation had died in the wilderness. But God was still with his people, ready to make a new beginning with those who trusted him.

In subsequent centuries when the people of God recalled their desert experience, they remembered it both as a time of trial and suffering and as a time of special closeness to God. For example, Jeremiah speaks of the intimacy between God and his people in the desert:

> I recall your youthful devotion, your bridal love,
> How you followed me through the desert,
>   through a land unsown [Jer 2:2].

And the psalmist speaks of Israel's rebellion:

> God's anger rose against them; he slew the strongest among
>   them, struck down the flower of Israel.
> Despite this they went on sinning; they had no faith
>   in his wonders. . . .
> How often they defied him in the wilderness and caused
>   him pain in the desert!
> Yet again they put God to the test and grieved the
>   Holy One of Israel [Ps 78: 31-32; 40-41].

To be true to the desert experience as the Old Testament describes it, we have to say that it was not only a time of intimacy and dependence on God but also a time of rebellion and strife.[8] However, the negative aspects were sometimes softened to the point that the desert experience came to be remembered as a golden age.

Golden age.[9] By glossing over the infidelities of the people of God, their desert experience can be idealized as a golden age of fidelity to God. The desert was the time when God was served with the purest worship, uncontaminated by the influence of the gods of Canaan. By the second generation, the people were untainted by idolatry; they knew only Yahweh as their God, and they were totally dependent on him. In later times the prophetic call for a return to the desert was a call to a new life of faithful service of God. Again and again the Israelites needed to remember that key situation of the first desert experience, so that they might renew their covenant with God. They looked to the desert for renewal, for a new covenant.

New covenant. Whenever the Israelites were oppressed, or exiled, or dominated by a foreign power, they began to long for another spectacular intervention of God in their history. They longed for a new exodus, a new law, a new covenant. They looked for a new prophet to lead them out of the desert of exile and bondage into the promised land of freedom and self-rule [Dt 18:15]. They longed for the day of the Lord, when God would act again and bring about a universal restoration of his people. Elijah, the desert prophet, was expected to return as the forerunner of the day of the Lord [Mal 4:5-6]. When John the Baptist appeared in the desert the priests and Levites sent a deputation to ask whether he was Elijah or the Prophet or the Messiah [Jn 1:20-21]. The salvation that the Israelites were expecting was linked to the desert [see Mt 24:26]. There was to be a new beginning, in the desert. Without knowing exactly how God would choose to act, the people were prepared to follow a new prophet who would lead them to political freedom.

Freedom. The freedom into which God was about to lead his people was a spiritual freedom, a freedom from sin, the freedom of the children of God. To have freedom is to have possibilities for the future, and the desert itself can be a symbol of the sovereign divine freedom and the infinite possibilities of the future that stretches out before us farther than the eye can see.[10] God liberated his people from slavery in Egypt and led them away from their familiar, limited past; he led them out into the uncharted freedom of the desert towards a new future rich with undreamed-of possibilities. The Israelites were constantly tempted to go back to Egypt, back to what was in the past even though the past was enslaving. God was asking them to trust him, overcome their fear of the unknown, and follow where he would lead them. The desert experience was not meant to last forever, but only until the mysterious, promised land was reached. God was asking his people to trust even when they could not see what lay ahead. Their desert experience was the experience of moving, in trust, through the harshness of the present into the mystery of the future; and God was their future.

It is in the light of the Old Testament desert experience as an historical key situation that we will look at the desert experience of Jesus and of the contemporary Christian.

PART B

DESERT EXPERIENCE OF JESUS

Desert experience can be a time of apparent abandonment by God. God seems to use the desert experience to test the depth of a person's trust in him and obedience to his plan; the test comes when God seems to withdraw his help and support, leaving the person on his own. The gospels describe three principal times of desert testing in the life of Jesus, as we will see in this section. The memory of the original desert experience of the people of God was part of the historical heritage of Jesus and helped him as man to live the mystery of his own desert experience.

Temptation in the Desert[11]

Jesus left his home in Nazareth of Galilee in order to receive John's baptism of repentance in the Jordan. As Jesus came up out of the water the Spirit descended on him and a voice was heard from heaven: "You are my beloved Son. On you my favor rests" [Mk 1:11]. When God led his people across the Red Sea he adopted them as his own sons, but the people took their sonship lightly and grieved their Father by repeated infidelities throughout their history. Jesus, however, was to be God's "beloved Son," the faithful son, the new Israel. Jesus' willingness to undergo baptism already signified his filial obedience and trust, but now his intentions were going to be put to the test in a confrontation with the adversary of God called Satan.

After the baptism Jesus was led by the Spirit into the desert. "He stayed in the wasteland forty days, put to the test there by Satan'' [Mk 1:13]. Jesus' desert experience is described in these simple phrases. Since Satan operates in the desert, being in the desert will often entail being put to the test by Satan.

The desert experience of Jesus was a struggle between the power and the plan of God present in Jesus and the power of evil personified in the form of Satan. The clash between these two forces only began during these forty days; it continued throughout Jesus' public ministry in his exorcisms, his healings, his instructions of the ignorant, his controversies with the Pharisees, and so on. The gospel of Mark does not describe the details of Jesus' struggle with Satan after his baptism because his whole subsequent ministry was an explanation of how Jesus was put to the test by Satan. The Spirit who led Jesus into the desert northwest of the Dead Sea led him also into the desert of his ministry where he encountered evil again and again. Desert experience became the leitmotif of Jesus' public life.

From time to time during his public life we see Jesus voluntarily withdraw into the wilderness to find relief from the press of the crowds and to refresh his spirit in prayer and silence. These temporary retreats usually come after a highpoint in Jesus' teaching ministry or after a miracle [see Mk 1:45; 6:32; Mt 14:13, 23; Lk 4:42]. We do not know what went on during those long hours of solitude, but we can see them in the context of Jesus' desert experience as the time when he gave God the glory for any successes, reaffirmed his filial obedience, committed himself again to his mission, and deepened his relationship as God's beloved son.[12]

The Agony in the Garden

The garden of Gethsemani was the scene of another desert experience in the life of Jesus [Mt 26:36-46; Mk 14:32-42; Lk 22:39-46]. His disciples went with him to the Mount of Olives, but Jesus left all but three of them in order to pray in solitude. At a certain point he left the three by themselves, telling them to stay awake and pray that they might not be put to the test. Jesus himself withdrew from them about a stone's throw and fell prostrate in prayer. There, on the eve of his passion, Jesus was alone. Knowing, or not knowing, all that was to come, he was in anguish; his heart was nearly broken with sorrow and distress. At that moment when everything seemed impossible for him, he prayed to the God of infinite possibilities:

> He kept saying, "Abba (O Father), you have the power to do all things. Take this cup away from me. But let it be as you would have it, not as I" [Mk 14:36].

Jesus repeated his prayer, but this time there was no voice from heaven to comfort him. Seeking the consolation of his friends, Jesus went back to Peter, James, and John but found them asleep. He was alone. Again he returned to his prayer, saying the same words. Still there was no comfort. He tried his friends once more but they were asleep. Back to the same prayer, then back to his friends a third time. This time he got them up, for his hour of destiny was at hand: "The hour is on us when the Son of Man is to be handed over to the power of evil men" [Mt 26:45].

Fortified only with the strength of his trust and obedience, Jesus went forth to the ultimate battle with evil and death. After the desert experience of Gethsemani, with its anguish and loneliness, Jesus had to face the desert experience of the cross.[13]

Jesus on the Cross

The cross was the culmination of Jesus' desert experience, the final test of his obedience and trust, and the moment of his definitive victory over Satan. Lifted up on the cross, Jesus was totally alone and helpless, cut off from human consolation and apparently cut off from God as well. The chief priests, scribes, and elders led the people in jeering at his helplessness: "He relied on God; let God rescue him now if he wants to. After all, he claimed, 'I am God's Son' " [Mt 27:43]. Had God truly deserted his beloved son? Jesus himself must have wondered, and that temptation to doubt and mistrust was Satan's last desperate effort to win possession of the new Israel. Both Matthew and Mark report that Jesus cried out in a loud voice, " *'Eli, Eli, lema sabachthani?'* that is, 'My God, my God, why have you deserted me?' " [Mt 27:46; Mk 15:34].

Jesus' cry from the depths of his desert experience was phrased in the opening words of Psalm 22. Regardless of whether Jesus went on to say the whole psalm or not, we are justified in saying that Psalm 22 articulates the experience Jesus was going through at that moment. The first part of Psalm 22 contains the words of a man in the desert experience:

My God, my God, why have you forsaken me?
You are far from my plea and the cry of my distress.

> O my God, I call by day and you give no reply;
> I call by night and I find no peace. . . .
>
> All who see me deride me.
> They curl their lips, they toss their heads.
>
> "He trusted in the Lord, let him save him;
> let him release him if this is his friend." . . .
>
> Do not leave me alone in my distress;
> come close, there is none else to help. . . .
>
> Parched as burnt clay is my throat,
> my tongue cleaves to my jaws. . . .
>
> O Lord, do not leave me alone,
> my strength, make haste to help me!

The second part of Psalm 22 breathes a different mood. We hear a note of confidence, a promise of praise, a spirit of trust that God has already intervened to save his servant. The psalm concludes on this upbeat:

> And my soul shall live for him, my children serve him.
> They shall tell of the Lord to generations yet to come.
>
> Declare his faithfulness to peoples yet unborn;
> "These things the Lord has done."

On the desert of his cross Jesus made the thoughts of Psalm 22 his own; and those thoughts move from the darkness of desertedness to the new dawn of trust and confidence. Somehow, in the heart of Jesus as he went through his desert experience on the cross, there coexisted a feeling of godforsaken desertedness and a feeling of filial trust. Luke's gospel records the attitude of confident trust when he tells us that the final words of the dying Jesus were from Psalm 31:

> Jesus uttered a loud cry and said, "Father, into your hands I commend my spirit." After he said this, he expired [Lk 23:46; Ps 31:6].

The two synoptics, Mark and Luke, each report one aspect of the total reality of Jesus' death on the desert of the cross.

While the synoptic gospels make a chronological distinction between Jesus' passion and resurrection, John's gospel sees the theological reality of a single salvation event. "For John, Jesus' exaltation in glory and his being lifted upon the Cross are aspects of one and the same thing."[14] In the mystery of the final moment of Jesus' life, there is a transition from earthly existence to transfigured life; for John's gospel, death is a resurrection.

Reflection

In the following two chapters I will have an opportunity to reflect further on each of the three principal moments in the desert experience of Jesus. At this point it is enough to understand that the desert experience of Jesus is an historical key situation for us today, just as the original desert experience of the people of God was an historical key situation for Jesus and remains one for us today. The experience of Jesus should be indelible in our minds, just as the archetypal experience of his people was for Jesus himself.

Jesus lived through a desert experience because he was

the new Israel entering into a new covenant on behalf of all mankind. The Israel of old had rebelled against God's leadership in the desert; they preferred to trust in themselves and depend on themselves as much as they could. But Jesus was the obedient and faithful son, the beloved son. He let himself be led by the Spirit into the desert and then into the world for a one-to-one struggle with Satan himself. Jesus followed, in obedience and trust, the plan his Father had for his life, ministry, and sacrificial death. Jesus was without fault in his desert experience, "tempted in every way that we are, yet without sin" [Heb 4:15].

In the garden of Gethsemani Jesus faced all the dread of the desert alone. His closest friends were asleep when he most needed them. When he was arrested in the garden his disciples fled; the shepherd was struck and the sheep scattered. Jesus had foretold this desertion:

> An hour is coming—has indeed already come—when you will be scattered and each will go his way, leaving me quite alone. (Yet I can never be alone; the Father is with me), [Jn 16:32].

But when Jesus prayed, "Take this cup away from me," the Father was silent.

It was during the hours he hung on the cross that Jesus experienced the desert in all its atrocious indifference to human misery. On the cross Jesus lost everything and became the utterly poor man, absolutely dependent on help from others. When he reached the end of his own resources he seemed to be abandoned by both men and God. On a low hill outside Jerusalem, "outside the gate, . . . outside the camp," Jesus died in solitude [Heb

13:12-13]. The cross was Jesus' solitude, his wilderness, his desert experience.[15]

Jesus has gone through the desert experience before me, and his experience is an historical key situation for me today. If I today am in the desert of daily routine, Jesus has passed that way before me, living nearly his whole life in the routine of commonplace manual labor at Nazareth. If I am in the desert of loneliness, Jesus has passed that way, for at the moment when he looked for the support of his friends in the garden of Gethsemani they were asleep and later they fled in fear leaving him quite alone. If I am in the desert of senselessness Jesus has been there too, for he experienced the farthest limit of meaninglessness and godforsakenness as he agonized in the desert of crucifixion.

But Jesus is more than a model and exemplar whose desert experience I can remember and reflect on as an historical event. The mystery of Christ is a contemporary reality, an ever present reality. And the story of my life is part of Christ's continuing story. My desert experience reproduces at this point of history Christ's own desert experience. My own desert is somehow a sharing in the desertedness and self-emptying of Jesus. His experience is a key situation for me.

Conclusion

In this chapter we have considered the historical situations of salvation history that seem to be the key to the deeper meaning of the desert experience today. God put Israel to the test in the desert. He promised that he could lead them through the desert to a land of freedom and plenty. But the Israelites wavered back and forth between trusting God's promise and doubting it. At the boundary of the new land the majority opted to go back to Egypt and live the rest of their life in the security of slavery. In punishment God made them wander in circles for forty years until the entire generation died and was buried in the desert. Only those who did not doubt, whose trust in God's presence and promise remained firm, were permitted to cross the Jordan behind Joshua and Kaleb. Only this remnant survived their desert test.

In the New Testament we saw how Jesus himself was put to the test. Jesus did not yield to the Tempter in the desert nor in Gethsemani nor on the cross. Jesus did not lose his filial trust in God even when God seemed distant and indifferent. In Jesus there came into existence a new people of God, obedient, faithful, trusting. As Christians we today belong to the new Israel in Jesus Christ. In him we have triumphed over the test of the desert experience. He has gone through the desert before us and for us; today he goes through the desert in us. "In a certain sense, it can be said that Christ is our desert. . . ."[16]

If we can see Christ as our desert we can understand how our own personal desert experience as Christians is always permeated, conditioned, and modified by the historical key situation of Jesus' desert experience. What we are going through in the desert is an experience Jesus himself has already been through, more totally and perfectly. In fact, our desert experience is a mysterious participation in that of Jesus, and it could be said that he experiences the desert in us. In our desert of daily routine or of loneliness or of senselessness we follow Jesus "outside the camp" to stand beneath his cross and share his bitter rejection by men and his mysterious abandonment by God. There our trust is put to the final test in the desert of doubt.

CHAPTER FIVE

THROUGH THE DESERT OF DOUBT

The spiritual life of someone destined to follow Christ in the desert experience is not always a matter of gently and peacefully growing in intimacy with God in an atmosphere of increasing security and consolation. In the desert I sometimes do not know what I want or where I am going or who I should trust. Uncertainty and doubt make me feel more and more deserted. I want to trust in God but when I cry out to him for help he seems absent. When I most need the support and comfort of his presence, I seem to be cut off from him for reasons I can not understand. This feeling of general bewilderment I call "the desert of doubt."

In the present chapter we will see how our spirit of trust is put to the test in the desert of doubt, and how we can avoid the trap of despair and can deepen our trust as we journey through this desert. Three aspects or areas of doubt will be considered at some length: temptation, detachment, and emptiness in prayer. Temptation throws me into doubt as I make the important choices of my life, the choices that determine what kind of person I shall be. The experience of detachment or self-stripping can make me doubt whether I will have any human dignity or identity left when the desert is finished with me. Finally, emptiness in prayer raises doubts in me about the faithful presence of God in whom I have placed my trust. Reflection on the experience of different Christians and of Christ himself will help us learn the secret of trusting, in the desert of doubt.

TEMPTATION

Wherever the Christian is tempted and thrown into doubt as he faces a lonely decision, there is the desert. Today we find ourselves tempted by the allurements of evil present within ourselves and within our society. So subtle are these allurements at times, we have serious doubts about whether a choice or an action is good or evil; we are pulled in different directions at once. Temptation arouses desire, and desire gives birth to sin [see Jas 1:15]. Nothing cuts us off from God and leaves us feeling empty and deserted more than sin. If we are frequently falling into grave sin, it is not surprising that our spiritual life should be a desert experience. We have been put to the test and have fallen.

But temptation, in its basic sense of "testing," does not always imply enticement to sin. Temptation may be encountered in a more neutral situation that could evolve either to sin and death or to life and growth. In this neutral sense temptation is an inevitable part of the human condition, a situation in which the quality of a person's life is assessed.[1] Temptation faced in the desert experience reveals what a person is made of, probes his weak spots, and tests the depths of his commitments and principles. Temptation can result in a purified and well-tempered personality or in a morally shattered and disintegrated life.

Temptation of St. Anthony

The temptation of St. Anthony is the classic model of desert experience temptation, complete with mythological trimmings. A third-century Coptic peasant, Anthony heard the gospel of the calling of the rich young man read in church and felt that the words were meant specifically for him. He promptly gave away his possessions and took up the ascetical life, going out into the desert where there was a cemetery with an empty tomb in which he could find shelter. Perhaps Anthony knew that the desert, and especially a cemetery, was the home of demons [see Mt 12:43]. But he trusted in God's assistance and was confident that he could provoke the demons in their own lair and be victorious with the help of divine grace. On cue the demons made their appearance and tried to frighten Anthony away by rushing at him in the form of wild beasts that howled and left his body racked with pain. Battered but undaunted, Anthony mocked the demons and called on the Lord. God did intervene but only after watching Anthony struggle for a long time on his own. When God finally appeared and put the demons to flight, Anthony asked:

> "Where were you? Why did you not appear at the beginning to stop my pains?" And a voice came to him: "Anthony, I was right here, but I waited to see you in action. And now, because you held out and did not surrender, I will ever be your helper and I will make you renowned everywhere."[2]

Anthony emerged the victor in this first encounter with the demons, but there were to be many more temptations just as fierce. In the desert Anthony learned to live with temptation, to expect it, to overcome it, and to experience the sustaining presence and power of God every time he called for divine assistance. For succeeding generations of monks and Christians, Anthony's combat in the desert became a model and a source of encouragement. What does his experience say to me today?

Reflection

Anthony's temptations seem foreign to the way I as a Christian experience temptation, but the structure of his experience is not so different from my own experience. I do not have to pass my nights in hand-to-hand combat with demons in the form of lions, wolves, and serpents the way Anthony did. I encounter temptations in broad daylight, in the form of things I hear, sights I see, situations I find myself in, and people I meet. When I recognize these external objects as temptations that may lead me astray from a wholehearted following of the Lord, then I can say No to them. Because they are external I can look at them, see them for what they are, reject them, struggle with them, as Anthony did.[3] But temptation may appear in a form so subtle I do not recognize it for what it really is.

I believe temptation comes more often from within me than from the world external to me. Even external temptations may seem temptations only because they correspond to an inclination already present in my own heart. It is possible to read St. Anthony's experience of demons as images projected or reflected from the desires present in his heart. Anthony may have been tempted in his heart to give up the ascetical life and run away from the desert; and the demons appeared in order to frighten him away.

Some of the temptations that rise within me are related to my flesh, and others to my human spirit. Among the former are temptations to laziness and letting things go, sensual indulgence, erotic inclinations, worry over my health, grandiose plans for the future. Temptations rising on the spirit level might include: bearing a grudge; angry, reproaching, and vengeful thoughts; boredom; fear; complacent vanity or smug pride; despair; self-pity; a craving for power over others. In the religious sphere, especially during a desert experience, there are temptations to stop praying, to doubt God's love, to compel him to break his silence and manifest himself. A more subtle religious temptation is the desire to promote God's kingdom on earth by Madison Avenue methods of salesmanship rather than by the methods and means employed by Jesus himself.[4]

I recognize within myself both the presence of evil and the presence of good, both the will to serve God and the reluctance to serve him. These forces within me are locked in perpetual battle.[5] I am not an observer on the sidelines as this struggle goes on within me; I have to take sides. I face the challenge of making a choice. I would prefer to make a compromise, or to dally with temptation, or to hold both poles in perpetual tension. I would postpone the choice because I am afraid I will not choose God. From past experience I know that when I choose I will probably yield to temptation. I cannot help myself. What I do not want, that I end up doing.

The experience of temptation makes me realize that I cannot hold out forever without God's help. Temptation brings me to the limit of my power of resistance. Temptation lays bare my essential weakness and vulnerability. What I know about the Old Testament desert experience teaches me that God permits temptation in order to see whether I will come to the point of acknowledging my complete dependence on him. In the temptation of St. Anthony, God stood by to see whether Anthony would call on him. "Anthony, I was right here, but I waited to see you in action."

The desert experience of temptation teaches me how much I need God's continual help. When I am tempted, I have to pray in words like these: "O God, help me! I am terribly tempted and can not hold out any longer. Please come and take control of me. Let me be tested no longer. But thy will be done." I may have to repeat my prayer again and again, as Jesus did in Gethsemani. I have to trust that God is present and that he loves me even when he seems permanently absent. Until he comes, I have to go on struggling and praying. God follows his own timetable in the desert experience. Anthony's first words, when God brought him relief, were: "Where were you? Why did you not appear at the beginning to stop my pains?" In Anthony's experience I see the principal lines of my own experience of temptation in the desert.

Temptation of Jesus

I have already touched on the episode of Jesus' temptations in the desert, but here I dwell on the subject because of the light it sheds on the Christian's current key situation of temptation. After his baptism, Jesus "was conducted by the Spirit into the desert for forty days, where he was tempted by the devil" [Lk 4:1]. The forty days Jesus spent in the desert recall the forty years of temptation and testing that Israel experienced in the desert of Sinai; where Israel had failed, Jesus stands firm. Mark's gospel does not describe the triple temptation; Matthew and Luke describe three temptations but reverse the order of the final two. Luke's version will be followed here. The order of temptations is not crucially important, as all three seem to be variations on a single theme. Commentators differ in their interpretation of the temptations of Jesus. I will present them as a challenge to Jesus's trust in God, an experience of the desert of doubt from which he emerged confirmed in his mission and his identity.

The first temptation prarallels the Israelites' complaint in the desert that they had no bread to eat [Ex 167:2-4]. "The devil said to Jesus, 'If you are the Son of God, command this stone to turn into bread.' Jesus answered him, 'Scripture has it, "Not on bread alone shall man live" ' " [Lk 4:3-4]. Jesus answered the devil's temptation by quoting Dt 8:3: "Man does not live by bread alone but by everything that proceeds out of the mouth of the Lord." Jesus is equivalently saying that bread is not so important. God can supply bread from heaven as he supplied manna in the desert. What is important is God's word, his law, his divine plan, the spiritual sustenance of which bread is the material symbol. To attempt to miraculously change stones to bread would be a failure to trust God's constant care or his plan to provide bread in his own time and manner. God will fill those who hunger for his will and his wisdom rather than their own.

The second temptation parallels the Israelites' fall into idolatrous worship of a golden calf at the foot of Mount Sinai [Ex 32:1-10]. The devil took Jesus up to a high place and promised to give him all the power and glory of the world, saying "The power has been given to me and I give it to whomever I wish" [Lk 4:6]. But Jesus refused to bow in homage to Satan, and he repulsed the temptation with a verse from Dt 6:13: "You shall do homage to the Lord your God; him alone shall you adore." Jesus did not refuse to accept all power and glory, for he eventually claimed such authority [Mt 28:18]. But he refused to have it in any other way than that ordained by his Father, even if the Father's plan meant obedient acceptance of death on a cross [Phil 2:8-9]. To accept the power and glory offered by Satan would be a failure to trust that the Father's plan truly did lead to glory even through the ignominy of the cross.

The third temptation parallels the many occasions when the Israelites put God to the test in the desert [see Ex 17:7]. This time the devil himself quoted scripture to tempt Jesus to throw himself down from the parapet of the temple. Psalm 91 promised that God's angels will watch over him and their hands will support him. "Jesus said to him in reply, 'It also says, "You shall not put the Lord your God to the test" ' " [Lk 4:12]. Jesus knew that God did care for him and would certainly support him, and he was content to live on in that untested trust in God. To deliberately throw himself from the parapet of the temple to see if God really would intervene would have been a failure to trust God's continual, unseen presence and protection.

All three temptations in the desert were attempts by Satan to make Jesus give up his trust in God and rely on his own plans, his own powers, his own freedom. Jesus, the new Israel, overcame the Tempter in the desert by his continual lived trust and dependence on God. The victory of Jesus over Satan constitutes an historical key situation for the Christian in his current desert experience of temptation.

Reflection

An early patristic text says, "It was not only Christ who was led by the Spirit into the desert but all the children of God who have the Holy Spirit."6 Jesus' temptation in the desert is an archetype of my temptations as a Christian in the desert experience. The story of Jesus' temptation is my own story as well. Basically what is that story? I have presented Jesus' threefold temptation as a crisis of trust in his Father. Each time he resisted Satan's temptation Jesus reaffirmed his strong, living trust in his Father, his Father's constant care and protection, his Father's plan for Jesus' life and mission.

In my life too, temptation is a crisis of trust in God and his plan for me. Temptation offers me a choice of having it my way or having it God's way. The enticement of immediate gratification makes me doubt whether God's way of self-forgetfulness and renunciation is the right way for me. I prefer the easy way, the path of least suffering and maximum gratification, the path that leads to prestige and power. I prefer to be in the promised land and not in the desert; that is temptation. Satan offered Jesus the promised land of plenty, but Jesus preferred the desert until God's Spirit should lead him elsewhere. The desert is God's way to the promised land. Jesus chose to entrust himself and his life to God's way. Jesus resisted the Tempter and placed himself in God's hands, with confidence and trust.[7]

Often I rely on my own wits and strength to remain unharmed in situations of temptation. And often I fall. Jesus in the desert did not trust his own strength far enough to use even his own words. Instead he answered Satan in the words of scripture, the word of God. Jesus relied on the words of power and life in scripture, not on his own words. As far as his own words or plans or desires go, Jesus is reduced to silence. The only defense he trusts in is God's word and plan and desire for him. Silencing his own word, Jesus conquered Satan with God's word and emerged from the test as God's spokesman. Only what he had heard from the Father did Jesus speak during the course of his ministry. Jesus left his own word and will there in the silence of the desert, and found instead a mature identity as God's spokesman, God's obedient and beloved son. In the desert Jesus came to himself before God because he chose obedience to God's mysterious plan.[8]

When I fall to temptation and disobey God's will, it is not because the devil, or anybody, made me do it. I am free to obey or disobey. I am able to resist temptation because Jesus in the desert resisted temptation for the whole human race, and it is in virtue of his victory that I can be victorious. Our first ancestor, Adam, fell to his temptation and was driven out of paradise into a land of thorns and thistles, a desert land. Jesus, the last Adam, was led into the desert in order to meet and conquer temptation, thus opening for us the way back to paradise. I have the option of following the disobedient Adam who ate the forbidden fruit offered by the Tempter, or of following the obedient Jesus who refused to turn stones into bread because it is not by bread that man lives. Man lives by trusting and obeying God in the desert of doubt and temptation.

The struggle with temptation is likely to last my whole life. As long as there remains some residue of the old Adam within me, I am prone to evil, and my hand reaches out easily in the direction of the forbidden fruit. But I have the radical power to pull back, thanks to the grace of the new Adam who freely stretched out his arms on the cross for my sake. Temptation exercises and strengthens my will-power so that I can say No to the choices that would place my pleasure before the will of God, and say Yes to the choices that would be my best response to the call of love in a particular situation. I may not have to do battle exteriorly with wild beasts as in *The Life of Saint Antony,* but I should be prepared to come to grips with the beasts inside me as long as I live.

As I journey through the desert of temptation and draw closer to the promised land, the temptations become more subtle and hard to recognize. Wild beasts are easy to identify; these are the gross temptations to acts of vice and violence. But the Tempter has many disguises. Will I recognize him under the form of misguided charity, arbitrary use of power, complacency with natural talents or spiritual charisms, and the repeated judgments that value money, time, and prestige more than people? The desert experience is meant to purify me at ever deeper levels of selfishness and pride, and to liberate me from all encumbering attachments. The desert strips away layer after layer of ego until my true self is exposed. The following section studies the process of self-stripping and detachment.

DETACHMENT

While temptation made me doubt about my choices and decisions, the desert of detachment makes me doubt about my very self. Detachment strips away the outer covering I had identified with my true self. As I experience this stripping away I doubt whether anything will be left of me at the end, whether any solid substratum of myself really exists.

In fact detachment is not a process of diminution but a process of liberation, through which the real me is set free from the layers and bands of material I have wrapped myself in for protection and security. Being in the desert experience is like being Lazarus in the tomb and hearing Jesus outside calling, "Lazarus, come forth." I come out but I am still "bound hand and foot with linen strips." So Jesus comands once more: "Untie him and let him go free" [Jn 11:43-44]. The difference is that in the desert experience I may feel the bandages being torn away but I do not hear who is giving the command and I do not know I am being liberated. I know only that I am being exposed, in all my vulnerability. The stripping lays bare my inner emptiness and desertedness; the process is terrifying.

Each person is held bound by his own tailor-made suit of defensive armor. My ambition and greed bind me and enclose me, as do my strong opinions and prejudices, my vain self-image, my little white lies, and especially all my fears. When I am liberated from my fears, then I am finally free. I have to submit to the stripping process of the desert experience until every covering is removed and the self that is being smothered inside is uncovered and brought to light. Then I can step forth like the resurrected Lazarus, in the emptiness and terror of my freedom, in the exposure of my inner openness, and in the vulnerability of my total trust.

The desert experience detaches. The desert simplifies a person's life down to the essentials. The things that matter any more are reduced to a few fundamentals. The physical desert, in its austere barrenness, is symbolic of emptiness, purity, freedom. The desert sun and wind have leveled this land, erased it like a giant chalkboard, and left it receptive to anything that wants to be written on it. The desert is ready to take on any form; its sand dunes may be molded and shaped in a myriad of ways. Such freedom is won at the price of total detachment.

Our reflections on detachment in this section will be based on a gospel example: Jesus' desert experience of detachment and self-divestment in the garden of

Gethsemani. In Gethsemani Jesus, in his complete freedom, took on the destiny that his Father willed for him. He stripped himself of his own will and was free to be molded and shaped according to his Father's will. Gethsemani was but a further degree of that process of self-emptying that began at the moment of the incarnation. As the letter to the Philippians describes it:

> Though he was in the form of God he did not consider equality with God something to be grasped at. Rather, he emptied himself and took the form of a slave, being born in the likeness of men [Phil 2:6-7].

Jesus in Gethsemani

On the evening of Passover Jesus knew that his hour was at hand. He led his disciples to a garden where they could be alone and he could unburden his heart to God in prayer. The hour was coming when he who had given so much of himself would have to give all, in fulfillment of his Father's mysterious will. Already he could feel himself being emptied out, and the uncomfortable emotions of doubt, sorrow, and distress rose within him [Mt 26:27]. Stark human fear, the fear of pain and death, clutched his heart and caused him to shudder. He said to Peter, James, and John: "My heart is filled with sorrow to the point of death. Remain here and stay awake" [Mk 14:34]. Then Jesus withdrew a short distance, fell to the ground, and cried out to God: "*Abba* (O Father), you have the power to do all things. Take this cup away from me" [Mk 14:36]. His prayer evoked no response from the Father. He who had confidently asserted, "I can never be alone," was very much alone at that moment. His Father was silent; his disciples were sleeping. "In his anguish he prayed with all the greater intensity, and his sweat became like drops of blood falling to the ground" [Lk 22:44]. There in Gethsemani the passion of Jesus began; it would not end until he had emptied himself of his last drop of blood [Jn 19:34]. There in the garden Jesus said Yes to his Father's will, letting go of his own deepest human instinct of self-preservation. He prayed, "But let it be as you would have it, not as I" [Mk 14:36]. The subsequent events of his passion and death were the unfolding of that definitive decision taken by Jesus in the garden, to renounce his own will in favor of his Father's way.

Reflection

If the hour comes when I am handed the cup of detachment to drink, I need to remember that Jesus himself experienced this before me. Having already emptied himself to take the form of a slave, Jesus in Gethsemani humbled himself still further and obediently accepted death on a cross [Phil 2:7-8]. Gethsemani was his desert.

The desert experience leads me to total self-emptying and detachment. The emptying process of detachment usually begins on an exterior level, but it ends in the depths of my heart. St. John of the Cross says, "Spiritually speaking, the desert is interior detachment from every creature in which the soul neither pauses nor rests in anything."⁹ In this reflection we shall see where the desert's call for radical detachment might lead us.

Detachment from things. I may first experience the call for detachment in the area of material possessions. If I place my security in money and the things that money can buy, I will never learn what it means to trust God [see Lk 16:13]. Even things of no great monetary value may separate me from God because I cling to them. A story from monastic tradition illustrates this point:

> Once there was a great saint who after forty years of ascetic discipline still could not reach God. Something stood in his way preventing him. At the end of forty years he understood. It was a little jug which he greatly loved because it cooled the drinking water he stored in it. He smashed the jug and was immediately united with God.[10]

Detachment is like a knife that cuts through the cords that bind me to things. The things I am asked to give up may in no way be sinful, but they bind me and inhibit my freedom. When Carlo Carretto entered the novitiate of the Little Brothers of Jesus he left everything behind but his address book. Then he took up the knife of detachment:

> . . . my novice master told me with the perfect calm of a man who had lived twenty years in the desert: *Il faut faire un coupure, Carlo*—(You have to make a break, Carlo). I knew what kind of cutting he was talking about and decided to make the wrench, even if it were painful.[11]

Carretto burned his address book.

My state of life as a Christian may oblige me to use and deal with many things, but detachment obliges me to do so non-possessively. I will deal with things without laying on the heavy hand of manipulation. I will try to use things respectfully, gently, freely.

Detachment from other realities. The same attitude of

non-possessive respect should characterize my relationships with other people, even the members of my family. If
my heart is cluttered with inordinate affections, the desert
will call me to detachment from my friends. I will have to
moderate my attachment to family and friends.

There are many impersonal, immaterial realities that I
may cling to as much as I cling to people and possessions.
The desert experience may call me to renounce grandiose
desires and fantasies, imaginary talents, dreamy illusions
in which I can accomplish everything. I will try to free
myself also from attachment to social status and to the
prestige of my community and country.

Detachment in religious matters. Sometimes I play a
game and try to fool myself into thinking that attachment
to church projects or liturgical matters or devotional prac-
tices is not attachment because I do these things for God.
Nevertheless even these things can keep me from God. The
desert detaches me from all that is not God, and even from
God himself insofar as I make of him an object to satisfy
my need for a comforting, guiding presence. There is a difference between God himself and the consolations of God;
for the sake of God alone I need to renounce the consolations of God in the desert experience.

Detachment can be compared to the weaning process.
The infant has to be weaned from mother's milk so that it
may grow to a mature self-reliance and independence.
God's comforting presence and consolations are food for
the infant stage of the spiritual life; the weaning process
begins when God leads me into the desert and withdraws
his presence so that I will learn to discern between the milk
and the mother. Then I will love the mother more than the
milk. My detachment *from* is always also detachment *for*
something else, in this case for God in himself.[12]

Christian detachment. What is left at the end of the process of Christian detachment in the desert experience? Will *I* even be left? The desert of detachment will strip away the false front, the social mask, the phony disguise, behind which the true *I* had been hiding.[13] The desert lays bare the true I, the I that is simple and poor, weak and needy, but created in the image of God. The desert dismantles the elaborate facade I had constructed to cover my creatureliness.[14] Detachment is a work of dismantling, disassembling, dissolving. The work of restoration that restores to me my true identity is like Ezekiel's vision of the scattered, dry bones which God brought back to life at the very moment when the Israelites were on the point of despair. The Lord spoke to Ezekiel:

> They have been saying, "Our bones are dried up, our hope is lost, and we are cut off." . . . I will put my spirit in you that you may live, and I will settle you upon your land; thus you shall know that I am the Lord [Ez 37:11, 14].

The desert experience of detachment culminates in the Lord's work of restoration and renewal that brings me back to my own land and my own true identity. If I trust in the life-giving power of God's spirit operative when I feel emptied, dried up, hopelessly poor, I will make a surprising rediscovery of all that I doubted I would ever see again. I discover myself and my world once again. Detachment and dispossession now appear as the path to true self-possession and the possession of all else in freedom and love. The emptiness of detachment wins me a kingdom. St. John of the Cross captures this paradox when he puts the following words on the lips of one who is detached from all but God:

Mine are the heavens and mine is the earth. Mine are the nations, the just are mine, and mine the sinners. The angels are mine, and the Mother of God, and all things are mine; and God Himself is mine and for me, because Christ is mine and all for me.[15]

Before I myself can make such claims, before I can say "God Himself is mine," I have to let go of everything but God himself. The familiar picture I may have of God is not God himself, and I will have to leave that image behind in the desert. God as he is in himself is wholly Other than I can imagine him, is transcendent Mystery. Likewise, my experience of God, whether in prayer or in my brothers and sisters, is not God himself. And so I will have to let go of my familiar forms of praying and of experiencing God as I journey through the desert. I can learn to trust him whom I do not name or experience, trust him because I love him. In the following section we will see how loving trust is tested in the desert of emptiness in prayer.

EMPTINESS IN PRAYER

Prayer does not have to be emptiness! For some people, and even for me sometimes, prayer is joy, love, and inexpressible fulfillment. "Taste and see how good the Lord is" [Ps 34:9]. At other times, prayer is the experience of my own inner poverty and the absence of God. The desert experience of emptiness in prayer is a journey into aridity and dryness, into the night of the senses, into the dark night of the spirit. Thomas Merton has described contemplative prayer as "simply the preference for the desert, for emptiness, for poverty."[16] I seek God alone when I pray, and God may lead me along desert paths or beside the restful waters of his consolation. Usually I have no choice; I pray from wherever I am.

I do have a choice between praying and not praying at all. In the desert of emptiness and dryness, the easy choice is to skip my meditation period. I tell myself I will make up for it later, when I am in the right mood for praying. I tell myself it is no use trying to pray when it would only be a meaningless exercise in endurance, with one eye on the clock. Behind my rationalizations lies a feeling of resentment. I am hurt. God seems to have let me down. He is not holding up his end of the bargain. If I am generous enough to give God half an hour of my time in meditation, he could at least give me a little encouragement. Priests and religious may be particularly susceptible to such feelings of resentment. We have abandoned all to follow Christ, but when it comes to prayer Christ seems to have abandoned us. We are left holding the bag, a bag of emptiness and desolation. So we skip the meditation. Besides, there are always the pressing needs of the apostolate. Why spend time in fruitless meditation when we could be responding to the call of charity in an active way that is often deeply fulfilling and meaningful to us?

In spite of the obstacles, prayer seems to be holding its own in the lives of priests, religious, and lay people in our country today. The popularity of such modes of prayer as Transcendental Meditation, Centering Prayer, Charismatic prayer, Zazen, and the Jesus Prayer all indicate a hunger for a deeper experience of God. People search for someone who can teach them to pray and guide them in the ways of the spiritual life. The retreat movement is flourishing in many parts of the country.

Many people are experiencing the need to withdraw temporarily from their everyday occupations and seek silence and solitude in order to devote themselves more exclusively to the Lord. A short time each day,or a longer time each week or each month, spent on retreat can bring a beneficial balance into a person's life and occupation. In the quiet of retreat he comes to terms with fundamental realities in his life, centers himself once again on the will of God, regains his physical, emotional and spiritual energy, and prepares to re-enter his everyday activities with spirit refreshed. A retreat can be a rejuvenating interlude of peace that strengthens us to face the duties of our Christian vocation even in adversity and suffering.[17] When the retreat stresses a simplified lifestyle in a setting of solitude and silence, it is sometimes called "a desert experience retreat."[18] We are fortunate today to have centers where desert experience retreats can easily be made.[19]

A temporary desert experience retreat dedicated to God alone is in no way detrimental to a person's commitment to his family, his community, or his loving service of others, any more than Jesus' occasional withdrawals to the mountain or desert detracted from his ministry. On the contrary, the retreat experience can enrich a person's ordinary life and activity. The more active a Christian is, the more he needs a periodic sabbath in order to be able to have something vital and substantial to give to others. We see the pattern of retreat-and-return in the lives of many creative individuals such as Jesus, Buddha, Muhammed, St. Benedict, St. Ignatius, Teilhard de Chardin, Hammarskjold, and others.[20]

I believe there is a healthy instinct, deep within our hearts, that periodically draws us to seek solitude, to seek the desert where we can be alone with God. That call of the desert was the propelling force that came upon Jesus after his baptism and on other occasions during his public ministry. The prophet Hosea heard the same compelling call spoken to Israel: "I will allure her; I will lead her into the desert and speak to her heart" [Hos. 2:16]. The habit of allowing time in our schedule for periodic desert days or desert hours will provide opportune periods when God may speak to our listening heart. With practice, our prayer of listening may become part of us, a prayer experience into which we can enter frequently during the course of an ordinary day. The essential desert is interior, within our heart. By entering the desert of the heart to adore God in a silent act of listening love, we can have a desert moment in the midst of our daily occupations, and in the company of other people.

Prayer becomes an all-pervading part of our life when we give free rein to the Spirit's sanctifying action in us. Once we have set out on the journey of periodic meditation, we cannot foresee where the journey will take us. In the present section our special interest is in the journey of prayer that has gone down a desert path into the experience of emptiness, aridity, and doubt. In this desert we can begin to doubt God himself. And as the desert experience is prolonged we eventually realize that there is nothing we can do to make anything happen in our prayer or to force God to reveal himself and remove our doubts. The Israelites had to spend forty years in the desert learning the lesson that there was nothing they could do to save themselves; their situation was fundamentally beyond their control and they had to place all their trust in a God who would provide for them and lead them day by day. In our own desert experience of emptiness in prayer we too will have to learn to accept and even prefer our state of helplessness, poverty, and nothingness so that God can fill us with his own fullness, in his own good time. To illustrate the desert of emptiness in prayer we turn to the private journal of a prominent Catholic woman who died only a few years ago, Raïssa Maritain.

Raïssa Maritain[21]

Until her journal was published, posthumously, few suspected the depth and intensity of Raïssa Maritain's prayer life. Prayer, which she called her *"oraison,"* was not one occupation among many others in her busy life but a constant awareness and availability for the word of God. Whether she was engaged in writing and editing, meeting and entertaining guests, or traveling and speaking, Raïssa Maritain was never far from her *oraison.* Yet God often seemed very far from Raïssa. She felt his absence and his silence like a physical pain. She felt that something was barring her way to God, cutting her off from his presence, imprisoning her so she could not approach him as she wished. In her journal entry of October 27, 1924, Raïssa wrote of her desert experience:

> I have suffered very much. God absent. The soul all crushed. Feeling this appalling void in my heart, I utter agonising cries inwardly. I feel as if there were nothing left to me but a scrap of faith, an atom of hope. I have lost all sense of liberty of heart. I feel a prisoner in a very rigid prison. This prison is open to the sky, I know that. But no one is there to raise me up from earth, and I am like a bird with broken wings. I drag myself about and everything hurts me [p. 174].

In spite of her painful feeling of desertedness and inner emptiness, Raïssa did not give up her trust in God. She continued to drag herself about in this desert, sustained by only a "scrap of faith, an atom of hope," and her great love. She did not doubt that her prison was "open to the sky," and release was possible. Five days later, on the Feast of All Saints, release did come in the form of spiritual consolation when she was able to participate in a Mass offered by a friend in her own home. Afterwards she reflected in her diary on the desert experience of the past few days:

> Truly I shall not call it living to suffer as I have suffered these last days. It ought rather to be called wandering on the threshold of death, experiencing nothingness, measuring the abyss of our solitude [p. 174].

But the time of consolation was not to last. God was not finished testing and purifying Raïssa in the aridity of the desert. Ten years later, Raïssa was still wandering in the land without hope. In an undated entry of 1934, she wrote of her aridity and emptiness:

> If anyone about me could taste only a little of this arid suffering, of this slow death, or the bitterness of these tears wrung from the very source of life—then they would understand. But I do not wish anyone such an experience [p. 230].

In her aloneness Raïssa felt that no one understood. Her husband was ever at her side, solicitous for her delicate health and for her peace of mind. Yet she felt desolate and no one could comfort her. Toward the end of 1934 Raïssa was coming to the idea that "existence in a barren desert" was part of her special vocation in life. Her way to God lay through the desert of almost continual emptiness in prayer, broken only occasionally at an oasis of consolation. The desolation and the consolation intertwined in confusing patterns that served to increase Raïssa's doubts. Sometimes God gave her consoling proofs of his nearness and his care in the midst of apparent absence. On such an occasion Raïssa wrote:

> Terrible ordeal in silent prayer. Felt all the bitterness of death. God asks of me more than my life: to accept living death, existence in a barren desert. That is giving more than one's soul. *Amaritudo amarissima.* Tortured, sobbing, I felt at the end, as it were, a faint whisper coming from the Lord. As if he were saying to me, "It is I, Jesus. You will find me again. Yes, you will do my will. Yes, you will accept it. Yes, you will be with me." The relief, the appeasement in which this prayer ended. But this *oraison* is all my life now. And death is proposed to me at every instant on God's side. I can accept it—and enter into the world of Jesus—or refuse it and begin to live the life of this world [p. 245].

In the midst of a terrible ordeal of barrenness and bitterness Raïssa seemed to hear "a faint whisper coming from the Lord," promising that she would be with him in the end. Peace and relief followed this assurance. Prayer was an ordeal in the desert, but Raïssa could not give up her prayer: "this *oraison* is all my life now." And every time she prayed she faced the bewildering choice of death or life—the living death of prayer in the desert of emptiness or the doomed life of a merely worldly existence. Raïssa conquered her hesitation and chose the desert path which, she trusted, would lead her into the promised land, "into the world of Jesus."

Reflection

We may not all be called to enter as deeply into the desert as Raïssa Maritain did, but I believe the experience of emptiness and aridity in prayer is fairly common in the spiritual life. This desert feeling may have many causes, not all of them due to God's action. For instance, I may experience a temporary period of aridity because of physical illness, fatigue, absorbing duties and responsibilities, and over-involvement in manual or intellectual labor. Also, I may find myself in the desert because of my own sinful attachments, infidelity to God's will, laziness, sensuality, pride, mediocrity, or negligence in prayer.

Yet there is an emptiness that is the work of God in my heart and leads to a beatifying communion with him in "the world of Jesus." It is the teaching of St. John of the Cross that union with God is often preceded by a desert experience of emptiness and doubt in prayer. "The soul," he writes, "must first be set in emptiness and poverty of spirit and purged of every natural support, consolation, and apprehension, earthly and heavenly."[22] Apparently this experience was the one Raïssa Maritain went through and the one that many others go through in their own measure.

It seems to me that there are two stages or degrees of the desert experience of emptiness in prayer, two deserts to cross. We may cross them successively or alternately or both at the same time; the distinction is useful only for purposes of description. The first desert might be called "the desert of truth" because it is here that I discover a more realistic and mature manner of relating to God, from the basis of my poverty and misery. I think there are many sincere and faithful people in the first desert, which corresponds to the night of the senses. The second desert, crossed by a smaller number, corresponds to the night of the spirit. Dereliction and anguish are experienced in the second desert, which might be called "the desert of God's silence." Let us reflect on both of these deserts.

Desert of truth. God leads me into the first desert in order to introduce me to a new way of experiencing him, through a purer faith and hope and love. Formerly I experienced God in a comfortably human way, as a person to whom I could relate and with whom I could converse as with a dear friend. I had a clear idea of God as a fatherly figure and could almost picture him in my imagination as I prayed. This way of praying was suited to my first efforts at meditation and contemplative gazing on the divine mysteries, and it brought me progressively closer to the truth of who I am and who God is.

When I am led into the desert of truth, I can no longer pray to God in my old familiar way; he is inviting me to relate to him in a way less dependent on images, concepts, ideas, thoughts, or mental representations. Slowly I discover that the obscure knowledge of faith and hope and love unites me more directly and intimately with a God who is beyond all my powers of comprehension. In the desert of truth I learn how to communicate with God in a dark, loving, intuitive, experiential mode of knowledge. Gone are the feelings of sensible sweetness tha I used to associate with the presence of God. Thomas Merton writes:

> Only when we are able to "let go" of everything within us, all desire to see, to know, to taste and to experience the presence of God, do we truly become able to experience that presence. . . .[23]

The desert experience of aridity in prayer, accompanied by an intense hunger and thirst for God alone, is a normal development in Christian spiritual life as God invites us to let go of our own satisfaction in prayer and reach for the love of him alone. St. John of the Cross is insistent that the desert way of aridity and emptiness is the only way to the knowledge and love of God in himself. Commenting on a verse from the *Psalms,* St. John writes:

> "In a desert land, without water, dry, and without a way, I appeared before You to be able to see Your power and Your glory" [Ps 62:3]. David's teaching here is admirable: that the means to the knowledge of the glory of God were not the many spiritual delights and gratifications he had received, but the sensory aridities and detachments referred to by the dry and desert land. . . . Hence the dark night with its aridities and voids is the means to the knowledge of God and self. . . . [24]

The first desert establishes me in the true knowledge of God and of myself. Through the experience of emptiness and aridity, I realize the truth about myself, the truth that I am unable to generate my own fervent experience of God, the truth of my own inner poverty and wretchedness and my total dependence on God. In this desert I finally surrender my arrogant self-confidence and my brash certitude to stand alone before God in my nothingness. At that moment, when my human misery confronts the divine mercy, I stand in my truest relationship to God. I discover him then as my maker, my redeemer, my leader, my beloved, my all. To discover God as my all is to freely hand over to him the direction and control of my life in the present and the future. He will lead me through the desert on paths I cannot see. For me it is enough to have trust and faith and love of him, even in his apparent absence. I am simply one who has, in Thomas Merton's words, "surrendered to God in the desert of emptiness where he reveals his inutterable mercy without condition and without explanation in the mystery of love."[25]

Desert of silence. In the second desert I advance to a new degree of desolation and aridity in preparation for a purer experience of God's mercy and love. If there was any support for me at all in the first desert, there is none to be seen or heard in the second desert. St. John of the Cross describes this desert experience:

> Poor, abandoned, and unsupported by any of the apprehensions of my soul . . . , left to darkness in pure faith, which is a dark night for these natural faculties, and with only my will touched by the sorrows, afflictions, and longings of love of God, I went out from myself.[26]

We should give full value to St. John's words "poor, abandoned, and unsupported." The second desert is, par excellence, the experience of desertedness and inner emptiness. I feel that God is not merely absent; I feel that he has rejected me. As John of the Cross says:

> What the sorrowing soul feels most is the conviction that God has rejected it, and with an abhorrence of it cast it into darkness. The thought that God has abandoned it is a piteous and heavy affliction for the soul.[27]

At times I cannot help complaining and even being angry at God for deserting one who would never desert him. Then I recall that I have deserted him, many times, by my sins. I resent his silence and rejection, but what else do I deserve?[28]

In the second desert I enter most deeply into the silence of God. Raïssa Maritain heard a comforting inner voice saying, "You will find me again. . . . Yes, you will be with me." But this word came only after she had prayed persistently and obstinately in empty silence. Such silence eats away at my courage to pray, mocks my deepest convictions, and tends to reduce me to despairing dumbness. One of the most consoling doctrines in the Judaeo-Christian tradition is that our God is a God who speaks, a talking God. On almost every page of scripture we read: "God has spoken . . . thus says the Lord." As long as God continues to dialogue with his people, there is no reason for despair. But in my desert experience I encounter only silence. I wish for a prophet whom I could ask, "Is there any word from Yahweh?" [Jer 37:17]. The persistent silence suggests that there is no longer a God who speaks, or that I have been completely abandoned by him. If I have the courage to continue praying, I must cry out to an indifferent desert of silence, cry out my "Abba, Father" in the silence. Theologian Karl Rahner believes that such a prayer would touch the "true and final essence of prayer." He writes:

> When we have seen all this and have the courage to speak into this silence which seems to devour us the words "Our Father," then only, I think, out of that which robs men today of their courage to pray, there really dawns upon us the true and final essence of prayer.[29]

True prayer is prayer offered in the desert of doubt and presented to an absent God. Such prayer confronts the mystery of God's absence and presence.

Absence and Presence

The experience of emptiness in prayer, whether in the first or the second desert, prepares me for a beatifying union with God where I will be totally present to him and he to me. I can experience moments of such union even in the desert. The Lord of the desert may withdraw his presence or manifest his presence as he pleases. In fact, the law of prayer in the desert experience seems to be a law of alternation: aridity alternates with consolation, God's presence alternates with his absence. But when I am in aridity and emptiness, I think it will last forever, and I forget the law of alternation. I forget that because of his utter transcendence God's silent distance from me can include his nearness, and his absence can include his caring presence.

What do I mean by God's "presence?" God's presence is his infinitely abundant, overflowing life that reveals itself as loving concern for all creatures. I have to stretch my imagination to think of even a fraction of the infinite number of ways God can be present to me. In the first place I can know by faith about God's presence everywhere in his creation; in the desert, faith may be my only access to the reality of his presence. Secondly, beyond bare faith, I can be aware of God's presence because I sense his kindness, love, and care for me as an individual. Finally, beyond that awareness, God may grant me a sensation of his presence in a felt, distinguishable, experiential way. Most of the time my awareness of God's presence will be the awareness of faith or the mysterious sense of his loving concern. And these modes of presence may be mistaken for absence. As Henri Nouwen remarks:

Although at exceptional moments we may be overwhelmed by a deep sense of God's presence in the center of our solitude and in the midst of the space we create for others, more often than not we are left with the painful sense of emptiness and can only experience God as the absent God.

Even though God seems absent, I love him. And perhaps my love for him is more pure in his absence because then it is unmixed with any self-satisfaction. Perhaps I find God more surely when I search for him in absence, because then I do not find a mere projection of myself. At any rate I know that what I perceive as absence is no obstacle to God. God can be present even as the absent one, and precisely as the absent one. God's ways of being present are infinite. In fact, no mode of presence can do him justice, or make him fully present as he is in himself. Thus, "in the end, presence reveals itself as absence," because I discover that this awareness of his presence is as nothing to the infinite reality of the living God.

Conclusion

God cannot be known and loved as he is in himself unless he is known as the incomprehensible and loved as unattainable. In the desert of emptiness and doubt, I know and love God as incomprehensible, unattainable mystery. The act that puts me in contact with God in the desert is an act of mercy on God's part and of trusting surrender on my part. When my trust is strong enough to surrender to the absence and the emptiness, I am totally available and open to God's mercy.

Trust transforms me in the desert of doubt. Before, life

was a tangled skein of questions, uncertainties, fears, and hesitations. I was involved in a gigantic project to rescue myself from my desertedness and inner emptiness. Now, life has become infinitely simple. I simply trust. God knows about my desert experience and he sees my heart. I place my trust in his care for me, a hidden but effective care which has not failed me yet. I come back again and again to the great promises and themes of salvation history, and my trust feeds on these words of scripture and grows to strong assurance: "The Lord, your God, . . . has been concerned about your journey through this vast desert. It is now forty years that he has been with you, and you have never been in want" [Dt 2:7].

Trusting, accepting surrender is the most creative response I can make in the desert experience. The chief obstacle to such a response is a persistant refusal to be led into the unknown. If I cling to the past and resist the emptying and purifying action of the desert, I prolong my ordeal in the desert of doubt. The following chapter will take up these possible responses in greater detail.

PART III

CREATIVE RESPONSES TO THE DESERT EXPERIENCE

INTRODUCTION

In the second part of this book we came to an interpretation of what is going on in the desert experience. We saw the desert experience in the light of Christian revelation in the Old and New Testament. Our reflections yielded the conclusion that God purifies his people in the desert and prepares them for a new and deeper intimacy with him, symbolized by the promised land.

All these insights remain on the purely theoretical level until they are assimilated and lived by people who are actually going through a desert experience. Insight and understanding need to be completed in action. In Part III of this book we face the practical question of what to do and how to respond in concrete situations of desert experience. Chapter Six will consider two possible responses to the desert experience, resistance and acceptance. Finally, Chapter Seven will reflect on creative responses to specific desert experiences in middle age, in times of illness and suffering, and in dying.

We shall see that the desert need not have the last word. The desert is not infinite. Only God is infinite. Nor can the desert experience last forever; only the kingdom of God lasts forever. When I begin to see beyond the desert experience, I can accept it, and by accepting transcend it. Creative acceptance puts the desert experience in its place and turns my gaze toward the promised land.

CHAPTER SIX

RESISTING AND ACCEPTING

We know now that the experience of desertedness and inner emptiness might be part of God's mysterious, providential plan to purify our loving trust in him and to draw us into intimate nearness. In this chapter we will study two contrasting responses to God's purifying action. A person has the choice of fighting God's plan for him in the desert experience or of cooperating with God's plan and learning the lessons that have to be learned in the desert. We can freely choose the response of resistance or the response of acceptance. The two parts of this chapter will consider each response in turn. Resistance will be considered first because resistance is quite often our first reaction to an ordeal such as the desert experience.

PART A:

I RESIST THE DESERT EXPERIENCE

Particular forms of resistance depend on variable circumstances of personality, past history, and present life situation. Nevertheless it is possible to describe general categories of resistance. The forms of resistance I may choose as a particular individual will be similar to the ways in which people have been resisting the desert experience throughout history. If we go back to the narrative of the Israelites in the desert we can already see the typical forms of resistance.

Israel in the Desert

Through their desert experience God formed the Hebrew refugees into a community, his own people, totally dependent on him for their survival and prosperity. But the Israelites balked and resisted almost every step of the way; they earned the reputation of being a stiff-necked and stubborn people. They had scarcely crossed the Red Sea when they began to grumble against Moses and Aaron:

> "The Israelites said to them, "Would that we had died at the Lord's hand in the land of Egypt, as we sat by our fleshpots and ate our fill of bread! But you had to lead us into this desert to make the whole community die of famine!" [Ex 16:3]

God granted them the favor they asked and rained down food from the sky for them to eat:

In the evening quail came up and covered the camp. In the morning a dew lay all about the camp, and when the dew evaporated, there on the surface of the desert were fine flakes like hoarfrost on the ground. On seeing it, the Israelites asked one another, "What is this?" for they did not know what it was. But Moses told them, "This is the bread which the Lord has given you to eat" [Ex 16:13-16].

The Israelites ate the manna, but still they complained. They longed for the plentiful and varied food they had in Egypt:

Would that we had meat for food! We remember the fish we used to eat without cost in Egypt, and the cucumbers, the melons, the leeks, the onions, and the garlic. But now we are famished; we see nothing before us but this manna" [Nm 11:5].

Then God sent them quail to eat, but they were not grateful for long. Desert living was not to their liking at all. They demanded water:

"Why have you brought the Lord's community into this desert where we and our livestock are dying? Why did you lead us out of Egypt, only to bring us to this wretched place which has neither grain nor figs nor vines nor pomegranates? Here there is not even water to drink!" [Nm 20:4-5].

So God worked another miracle: "He pierced the rock to give them water; it gushed forth in the desert like a river" [Ps 105:41]. Moses took his staff, struck the rock twice, and suddenly there was water enough for the whole community and their cattle as well [Nm 20:11].

Each stage of the Israelites' journey was marked by similar protests and by God's intervention to supply their essential needs. God punished his people for their failure to trust him, but he never abandoned them in the desert. He responded with fidelity to their infidelity. As often as they repented he forgave them. Eventually, when they had learned to trust him, he led them to the promised land:

> They wandered in the desert, in the wilderness,
>> finding no way to a city they could dwell in.
> Hungry they were and thirsty;
>> their soul was fainting within them.
> Then they cried to the Lord in their need
>> and he rescued them from their distress;
> And he led them along the right way,
>> to reach a city they could dwell in [Ps 107:4-7].

Reflection

The stiff-necked and hard-hearted Israelites are not altogether unlike me as a Christian. I can almost sympathize with them in their plight, knowing that I might have acted in a similar way. I see myself in their hopeless feeling that they were never going to get out of the desert. I see myself in their incurable nostalgia for Egypt, for the good old days of the past when things were so much better. I can even see myself in their constant complaining and murmuring and protesting.

"Complaining" is perhaps the most characteristic aspect of the Israelites' resistance to their desert experience. Why did they continually complain and grumble against God? Like them, whenever I find myself in an unpleasant situation my first reaction is to change the matter somehow;

failing that, I try to get away from the situation or get out of it somehow. The Israelites could neither change the desert nor leave it. They found themselves thrown into an impossible situation which they could do nothing about. They could not help themselves. There was no possibility of living off the land. They did not know the way out of the desert. They were frustrated on all sides. The whole ex· perience was a meaningless waste. And so they complain· ed. Grumbling is the response of those who are unable to do anything else. Grumbling is a response made in utter frustration.

The Israelites complained chiefly about food and water, the things they needed most and could not procure for themselves in the desert. But these complaints about primary needs were symbolic of their dissatisfaction with the entire experience of being in the desert at all. The desert was God's way of bringing them to a state of total dependence on him, and trust in him. The longer they complained and refused to surrender to God, the longer the desert experience lasted.

The desert experience seems to have destroyed my more or less satisfactory relationship with God. Now he is maddeningly absent and I wonder what is going on in my life. Have I been duped by theologians and spiritual writers into thinking that I can find any fulfillment at all in an interior life? Is it worth going on like this, through a desert?

In this situation I can resist the purifying action of the desert experience by letting myself fall into lassitude and inertia, refusing to try any longer, settling for anesthetized mediocrity. Or else I might give in to despair, indulging in morose self-pity, hating myself and life and God. Or I can blame God for treating me so unjustly, for punishing me when I do not deserve it, for being arbitrary and high-handed when I have tried to serve him faithfully all my life.

A common form of resistance, when I feel myself losing contact with God in the desert, is to cling to the past or try to return to the past. As the Israelites longed to go back to Egypt, I long for the caresses and consolations I used to experience in prayer. In a desperate effort to recapture that sense of God's nearness, I stick slavishly to my familiar prayers and devotions, my tried and tested style of piety. I reread the devotional books and lives of the saints that were such an inspiration to me when I first began to pray. But now they seem remote and foreign, even silly.

When I do not at first succeed in rekindling my former fervor, I can take a deep breath and try harder, and then harder. Trying too hard is also a form of resistance. Either I think that nothing will happen in my spiritual life unless I do it myself, or I think that I can say the magic prayer and force God to be present. But all my favorite prayers are now like ashes in my mouth.

Perhaps the most common form of resistance is turning to something that will take my mind off the desert experience. I try to forget the whole thing and lose myself in more immediately satisfying activities. I fill up my inner emptiness with a myriad of experiences that never satisfy me very long. I move faster and faster in order to leave behind the desertedness feeling that comes whenever I slow down. I never let myself be physically alone for any length of time. I never let myself be unoccupied. I throw myself into a career, an assignment, a creative undertaking. I busy myself doing many great and good things for the honor and glory of God, so that I may never have to sit down and face his absence in the desert.

All these are forms of resistance to the desert experience. Some are obvious and deliberate, others are more subtle, more preconscious. In the desert resistance ultimately proves futile, but I can play the game of resisting for a long time and in many different variations before I come to realize the futility of it. The desert cannot be tamed by resisting it but only by loving it. God cannot be controlled but only obeyed or disobeyed. I, by resisting, cannot make my desert experience come to an end but can only prolong it that way. Eventually I will have to step out of the driver's seat and begin to acknowledge and to accept what I have refused to face.

Resistance is a normal and frequent response to the desert experience. But God is patient with me. Many of the most important lessons of life, both social life and spiritual life, have to be learned by experience, by trial and error; no one can learn these lessons for me. Resistance may be my initial response to the desert experience; perhaps only later, if at all, will I discover that the response of loving, trusting acceptance is far more productive. The movement from resistance to acceptance begins when I as a Christian can look with compassionate, rather than with critical, eyes upon my own divinely sustained, guided, and cared-for self in the desert experience.[1] When my trust in God outweighs my fear of desertedness and emptiness, I begin to move from resistance to acceptance.

PART B

I ACCEPT THE DESERT EXPERIENCE

God guides his people through the desert. He will never permit me to be tried beyond my strength, or to experience desertedness and emptiness beyond my limits of endurance. And it is God who sets the limits of my endurance and who gives me the grace to accept and cooperate with my desert experience. So much am I dependent on divine grace to perform acts leading to salvation, that it is only by his grace that I can respond to him with loving acceptance and trust. It is by the power of God's grace and his Holy Spirit present in me that I can say Yes to his apparent absence in my desert experience.

Are there any models for me as a Christian to think of when I try to make an accepting response to my desert experience?[2] In the first part of this section we will look once more at the figure of Jesus, the supreme exemplar of our spiritual life. The remainder of the section will reflect on examples of acceptance in the lives of people who have followed Jesus.

Jesus on the Cross

Jesus died on a cross outside the city, an outcast, rejected by his own people and apparently also by his own Father. Both Matthew and Mark report that Jesus spoke at least the opening words of Psalm 22 as he hung on the cross:: *"Eloi, Eloi, lama sabachthani*? which means, My God, my God, why have you deserted me?"* [Mk 15:34; cf. Mt 27:46]. This cry was wrung from the anguished depths of Jesus' heart at a moment that might be called his ultimate desert experience. Jesus knew that his Father was not distant but close at hand. Yet his Father would not intervene, would not come to the rescue in a show of power. Jesus felt abandoned and forsaken by the God whose faithful love endures forever [Ps 136, refrain]. Only Luke's gospel tells us of Jesus' other word from the cross, borrowed from Psalm 36. Here is not the tormented cry of a despairing man but an announcement of loving trust: "Jesus uttered a loud cry and said, 'Father, into your hands I commend my spirit.' After he said this, he expired" [Lk 23:46]. At that ultimate moment, Jesus responded to his desert experience with a cry of loving, trusting acceptance that also came from the anguished depths of his heart. God did not spare his own Son but gave him up for us all, so that "all the godless and the god-forsaken can experience communion with him."[3] The god-forsakenness of Jesus on the cross was simultaneously the moment of his deepest conformity and closest communion with his Father's will. The desert of the cross both separated and united Jesus with his Father to the maximum degree imaginable.

Reflection

When we reflect on the moment of Jesus' death we do so with the greatest reverence and respect because we confront here a mystery that is beyond our comprehension. For the sake of bringing the whole human race into the beatifying presence of God, Jesus endured the experience of God's excruciating absence: "My God, why have you deserted me?" The cross was a moment of dreadful dereliction and solitude for Jesus, yet "God was never nearer His Son than when He cried out from the cross that He had been abandoned.'"⁴ We stand in wonder before this mystery.

I think we have to give equal importance to these two words of Jesus on the cross, not stressing one more than the other. By keeping both poles of his experience together, we stay faithful to the full truth of that incomprehensible moment. Jesus truly felt deserted by his Father.⁵ Yet so great was his trust that his Father would never desert him, he could confidently commend himself into his Father's hands with his dying breath. Jesus could discern the loving presence of his Father in spite of and beyond the doubt that rose from the felt absence of that Father.⁶

We know how the loving trust of the dying Jesus was gloriously vindicated in his resurrection from the dead. Death and resurrection were two sides of the same event in Jesus' life, an event that John's gospel calls "exaltation" [Jn 3:14; 8:28; 12:32]. The answer that Jesus cried out for on the cross was given to him at the moment of his exaltation, when he died into risen life. Jesus' hour of desertion was transformed into his hour of victory. When he arrived at the outermost limit of desertedness and emptiness, Jesus found the glory of God and was taken up into that glory. When he let himself go and dropped into the abyss of death, his Father's loving arms welcomed him to everlasting, beatific life. In the dying Jesus we marvel at a sublime act of loving trust by which he entrusted the totality of himself to a mysterious, hidden, silent, incomprehensible Other who waited somewhere over the horizon of death.⁷

Because of Jesus' trusting acceptance of God in his hour of death, there is no desert experience so abandoned and empty that it cannot be accepted by a Christian in an act of loving confidence that will transform the very meaning of the desert. Just as Jesus discovered his Father's presence at the moment of most total absence, so the Christian may discover that his desert experience was a time of special nearness to God. Here we again come upon the paradox that desert experience can be a time of intimacy with God as well as a time of purification; the purification is ordered to the intimacy. In the act of acceptance, the desert is transformed into a promised land, and death is transformed into life. By acceptance of my desert experience I enter into the mystery of Jesus' victory over death and the desert on the cross. In my act of acceptance, he who went into the desert with me now triumphs victoriously in me.

Acceptance by Christians

It is not too difficult to find concrete historical examples of Christian acceptance of the desert experience. Still, everyone's response will fall somewhat short of the ideal, despite his best will and effort. Acceptance often alternates with forms of resistance in a normal rhythm of progression and regression that characterizes human development in the spiritual life. Instead of taking examples from the lives of the saints, who might be considered too heroic to imitate, I will select two examples from the lives of people who have not yet been canonized.[8]

Jean-Pierre de Caussade. Our first example is an eighteenth century French priest who was the proponent of a special spirituality centered on abandonment to divine providence. Abandonment for de Caussade meant a perfect submission in faith, hope, and love, to the will of God manifested in the present moment. In the course of his life, de Caussade had to practice abandonment as well as write about it. His desert experience began when he was transferred from the city in which he had established a large following to a city where he was completely unknown. In the following letter we can see his response of acceptance:

> I learn by [the isolation in which I live] to die to all things in order to live to God alone. I was not so shut away at [my former city]. There, many events both within and without kept me up, and made me feel alive; now, there is nothing of that kind. I am in a veritable desert alone with God. Oh! how delightful it is! Great interior desolation is joined to this exterior solitude. However painful to nature such a state may be, I bless God for it because I have no doubt that it is good for me. It is a universal death to all feeling even about spiritual matters, a sort of annihilation through which I must pass in order to rise again with Jesus Christ to a new life, a life all in God, a life stripped of everything, even of consolation, because in that the senses take part. God wishes to leave me destitute of all outward things, and dead to all to live only to Him. May His holy will be done in all things, and for ever![9]

De Caussade found himself in "a veritable desert" consisting of interior desolation and exterior solitude. His faith told him that he must pass through that death in order to rise to a new life. And so he prayed, "May His holy will be done."[20]

Walter Ciszek. Our second example is from the life of a contemporary Jesuit missionary who spent five years in solitary confinement at the Lubianka prison in Moscow. In his prison desert experience Ciszek first went through a period of self-confidence and reliance on his own strength to stand firm and meet every challenge. Under the pressure of brainwashing Ciszek eventually broke down and signed a confession. His failure at that critical moment was an experience of humiliation and purification that left him "cleansed to the bone." He began to move toward an attitude of deep trust and total dependence on God. He now saw that in his experience it was not God who had deserted him but he who had deserted God. Ciszek reflected on the denial of Christ by Peter, and wrote:

> I find it perfectly understandable that Peter, in his letters to the early churches, should have reminded his Christians to work out their salvation in fear and trembling. For just as surely as a man begins to trust in his own abilities, so surely has he taken the first step on the road to ultimate failure. And the greatest grace God can give such a man is to send him a trial he cannot bear with his own powers—and then sustain him with his grace so he may endure to the end and be saved.[11]

Reflection

I see in the lives of these men something specifically Christian about their acceptance of the desert experience. The response of perfect acceptance is so far above our natural human powers that it could only be the work of grace and the Spirit of Jesus within us. Seen from the perspective of faith, Christian acceptance of the desert experience is a participation in Jesus' own acceptance of his desert experience. The mystery of Christ is not confined to a limited period of history in the first century, but is a living, trans-temporal event that is contemporary with the lifetime of every Christian in every century. St. Paul could say, "I live now not I but Christ lives in me" [Gal 2:20].

And the Christian can say, "It is now not I who accept this desert experience but Christ who lives it and accepts it in me."

When we look closely at Christian acceptance of desert experience the characteristic quality of this acceptance seems to be its attitude of living trust in the triune God. In acceptance I trust in the triune God: in the Father who is always with his people; in the Son who went through a desert experience himself; and in the Holy Spirit who dwells forever in the hearts of the faithful. I trust in the Trinity's unfailing love and concern for me individually, as the three divine persons draw me into ever closer intimacy with themselves. The triune God leads me into the desert to teach me to live for him alone and to have confidence in him alone, in the sense of making him, and not myself, the ultimate center of my life and hope. The desert experience tests, purifies, and strengthens my trust in the loving nearness of God even when he appears to be absent or unloving. To place my trust in God despite desertedness and inner emptiness is the Christian response of acceptance and cooperation in the desert experience. In this concluding reflection I will explore some of the dimensions of trusting acceptance.

Trust in God's presence. To accept my desert experience is to trust that God is present even when he seems absent. There is a charming anecdote in the Old Testament that illustrates how God is present to his people and hears their cry in the desert. Hagar and her infant, Ishmael, were wandering about in the desert of Beersheba after they had been expelled from the house of Abraham. When her supply of water ran out, Hagar thought that she and her baby were doomed. She lay the infant in the shade of a bush and moved some distance away, "For," she said, "I cannot bear to see the child die'' [Gn 21:16]. The boy's crying was heard in heaven and God sent his angel to rescue them. The angel said to Hagar:

> "Don't be afraid; God has heard the boy's cry, even where he is. Arise, lift up the boy and hold him by the hand; for I will make of him a great nation." Then God opened her eyes, and she saw a well of water. She went and filled the skin with water, and then let the boy drink. God was with the boy as he grew up. He lived in the desert . . . [Gen 21:17-20].

In my own desert experience as a Christian, I want to trust that God is always present and that he will hear my cry and answer me "even where I am," even in the desert. It is easy to trust that God hears the worship offered him at a solemn mass in a splendid cathedral, but I have to trust that he is listening even in the arid desert. In times of consolation I may sense his nearness, but I have to trust that he is present even in times of aridity and emptiness. Sometimes the only prayer I can offer him is the prayer of my emptiness. I have nothing at this moment but my emptiness, so I offer that as my prayer. I trust that God will receive my prayer and that my longing for him in the desert will become a new mode of experiencing his nearness. May my trust be strong enough to embrace this emptiness, for it is the emptiness of God![12]

Trust in God's care. I trust not only in God's hidden presence but also in the caring and benevolent quality of his presence. And I trust in God's care for me more than my own care for myself. In order to come to total trust in God's care for me, I may have to be placed in a situation where I am totally unable to care for myself. God brought afflictions on his people in the desert and let them experience hunger in order to show his care for them by providing manna for forty years: "that he might make you understand that it is not on bread alone that man lives, but it is on everything produced by command of the Lord that man lives" [Dt 8:3]. In the desert land of insecurity the Israelites learned to depend on a daily dole of bread from heaven. There was always enough, but never more than enough, never so much that they could feel secure and forget their total dependence on God. In my own desert experience I want to trust that God will always provide for me. I trust him even when I am at the end of my resources because it is at that moment that the power of God is revealed.

There may be times when my trust is badly shaken because the manna God sends me in the desert experience does not look like bread from heaven at all. I looked for sweet-tasting bread but God has provided the "bread of tears" or the "bread of ashes" [Ps 42:4; 80:6; 102:10; Is 30:20]. I know that beggars cannot be choosers. Can I truly live by *everything* that proceeds from God's will and command? I need the trust to taste and see. If I truly trust in God's care for me I will see that everything in my life is bread that unites me to him in the mysterious sacrament of his love. Whatever he sends me is truly bread, and I can live from it in the desert.

Trust as waiting. If I trust enough in God's caring presence, I will wait in confidence for him to manifest himself and speak to me again even when his silence seems eternal. The physical desert seems in its silent immobility, to be eternally waiting; the desert is a land suspended in expectation, ever hopeful and ever unfulfilled. The physical desert is waiting for rainfall. Rain is God's good gift, the sign of his favor and blessing. As the desert waits for God's blessing, I too must wait in the desert experience. The desert experience tests my trust in God, and nothing can replace the test of time. So I must wait in the desert until my trust is purified of the last trace of self-reliance. The Israelites spent forty years in the desert until they learned to rely on God alone.

To accept my desert experience is to wait for God trustingly and confidently. Acceptance means I have to be patient with God as well as with myself. Acceptance means calm perseverance and long-suffering in the desert. I trust God's mysterious plan for my life. God has put me in this desert place for a reason best known to him alone. I accept his will for me, I accept the place where he has now placed me, I accept the desert experience. I know that I will not find God by fleeing from the desert but by letting him lead me across the desert to himself. And I know that I cannot compel God to speed up the desert stage of my journey. I must wait for God's plan to unfold in his own good time. In patient trust I go about the duties of my daily life, living life as it is given to me from my Father's hands. I wait in hope for the appearance of the Lord of the desert, sensing that he is already at hand giving me the power to wait in hope. I accept this present moment of desert experience and pray for the strength to accept the next moment. In the words of the prophet Micah, "I shall wait confidently for the Lord; I shall hope for the God of my deliverance; my God will hear me!" [Mi 7:7].

Conclusion

Acceptance of the desert experience is not a response that comes quickly and easily to human nature, but one that is always a living possibility with the help of God's grace. Trusting, loving acceptance makes it all one whether we are in consolation or desolation, dried up by the desert sun or refreshed by divine dew.[13] What counts is that our hearts remain centered on God alone, even in our desertedness and emptiness. What counts is living in the truth of things, in the desert reality of my present situation. I no longer attempt to escape or deny the way things and people and situations really are. Instead I accept my desert experience, accept both the searing harshness and the searing beauty of life in the desert. Both the harshness and the beauty are embraced by the love of the Lord of the desert, in whom I have put my trust.

In the following chapter I will test the strength of these conclusions against some of the more demanding desert experience situations in people's lives: the desert of middle age and the desert of suffering and death.

CHAPTER SEVEN

LIVING AND DYING IN THE DESERT

In this concluding chapter my concern is to bring down to earth all that we have learned about spirituality and the desert experience. Principles remain inoperative until they are inserted into real life and history, in response to actual needs and actual questions. Can the principles and truths learned in the foregoing chapters be applied to concrete life situations of actual people living today?

The situations selected for discussion in this chapter are common enough to be the experience of a large majority of people. Each individual goes through his own tailor-made desert experience, but there are certain life situations that potentially constitute a desert experience for most people. Here we will consider desert experiences that are related to the life cycle: the experience of middle age and the experience of suffering and death. A final section will emphasize once more the possibility of traveling through the desert in a spirit of cheerful trust, with eyes fixed on the promised land ahead.

PART A

THE DESERT OF MIDDLE AGE

People in their forties may begin to go through a middle age crisis that resonates throughout their social, biological, and spiritual life. After we cross an indefinite but clearly felt mid-point, our physical life starts its slow decline toward death. The range of possibilities still realistically available to us in life narrows progressively. The crisis affects our vocational and personal commitments, our certitude about decisions that have shaped our life, and our relationships with loved ones and with God. It becomes necessary to reassess our life orientation and reinterpret our position and place in the world. The world at this time of life can take on the bleakness of a desert. We shall examine this experience rather closely and then reflect on the creative response that it calls for. This description and reflection will be placed in the general context of religious, monastic life, but the reader may easily adapt it to the context of married or single life. The middle age crisis is no respecter of persons or life-styles.

Middle Age Crisis[1]

Developmental psychology looks at human life as a dynamic process of growth, extending all the way to the moment of death. The feeling of expansive, outward growth fosters a quality of zest for living that is characteristic of the majority of people until around their early forties. In the middle age crisis a person is confronted in a definitive way with limits to his life project of growth and expansion. He is brought up short by these limits and thrown back on himself. We call this stage of life the middle age crisis of limits. A person's zest for living may at this point be replaced by a more or less acute malaise and depression, unless he discovers new directions for life, growth and expansion. At first he wonders what is going on in his life. Everything that worked so smoothly for him in the past no longer seems to work. The world around him seems to be whirling faster and faster, just when he wants everything to stop for a moment so that he can take stock of the situation. The community he has been living in all these years now seems to be changing at a bewildering rate, as if it were rushing past and leaving him behind. Persons who were once very close to him seem to be drifting away from his life. Perhaps he has lost one or both of his parents. He sees some of his confreres, not much older than himself, getting their first heart attack, or arthritis, or diabetes, or cancer. The newcomers, with their peculiar ways, are a mystery to him, except for the fact that they seem to have an eye on his job. He reacts by hanging on more tightly to the power he does have, even though he is not sure how much longer he can stay on top of all his work. If he loses this job, what will he do? He wants to remain productive and dreads being put on the shelf and forgotten. Who should he speak to about all these concerns and anxieties when he himself does not know whether to take them seriously? What is going on?

The aging self. On each of the three dimensions of his life—vital, personal, and spiritual—the middle aged monk is discovering his limits. Physically he is changing and he has to admit he can no longer do the things he did a few years ago. The hormone production levels in his body are dropping, and his hair is thinning or turning gray. His waistline soon expands if he does not watch his diet. He has to admit that he has passed the peak of his physical resistance, resilience, flexibility, endurance, vitality. Old age and eventual death are now visible on the horizon. He is afraid to acknowledge that he has begun to slide downhill and there is nothing he can do to stop. The very thought of the end makes him uneasy.

On the ego-personal level, the dimension in which he evaluates himself and others evaluate him, it seems that his core sense of competence and worth as a man and as a monk is being challenged. Whether other people know it or not, he feels that his self-esteem, his self-image, is receiving heavy blows from all quarters. Although he is successful in some ways, he sees that in many ways he is a failure. Beneath the successes he now begins to discern an underlying layer of egoism, pride, sensuality, aestheticism. Sometimes he catches himself playing phony games and posing as an authority on things he knows very little about. Now he can see through the sham, the play-acting, both in himself and in others. More and more often he finds himself in a mood of sadness and depression, disenchantment, disappointment, loneliness, self-pity. He used to be able to sail through the day and through his work, but now time drags and a monumental fatigue weighs him down. At the same time something makes him restless, as if he were tormented by a nagging itch from head to heel. The normal frictions of community life bother him more than they should, and he finds himself losing his temper. He is aware that he is becoming hard to live with but does not know what to do about it. After what he has been through he has a right to be somewhat cynical. He feels he has cause enough to complain about life in general and about a few bothersome people in particular.

Finally, on the spirit level—the dimension of his being where he is free to embrace life-goals and ideals and projects—on that highest human level he has doubts and questions. Nothing is clear any more. He wonders, "What am I anyway? What am I doing here? What is the meaning of all this?" It is a time of self-questioning, a time of reappraisal of his aspirations in life. He spends meditation periods reviewing his life, looking back on his limited achievements, surveying the course he has taken. Can he honestly go on honoring a commitment made so many years ago to this life-style and this community? He wonders if he can be satisfied going on this way for the rest of his life. Perhaps he should do as so many others have done, and get out through the front gate while there is still time. But perhaps it is already too late to make a beginning anywhere else. It would be safer to stay where he is, stick it out in familiar surroundings, and make the best of what remains of his life. What has become of those high ideals he had when he entered the monastery? What has become of his faith? Even here doubts and questions seem to arise. Can any collection of dogmas give genuine meaning and purpose to a man's life, or is he laboring under illusion and self-deception?

Adjustment modes. How do people react to their middle-age crisis? How can a man revitalize all that has gone stale in his life? Some never find the key to a good adjustment; they get permanently stuck in a depressed, cynical, irritable, lonely, alienated, frustrated mood. They stagnate, become bored, and infect those around them with the gloom of their own intolerable weariness of life.

Other people can turn their middle age crisis into an occasion for true growth and maturation. They discover a new direction in which to channel their life energy. Instead of dispersing their energy outward, and continually running into limitations, they reflectively turn their attention within and grow in depth and interiority. For them the middle age crisis of limits has become a creative opportunity for growth, but in an inward more than an outward direction. Acknowledging their physical limits they try to keep body and mind in good condition, well-exercised, and disciplined. Psychologically, they know and accept themselves as they are, with all their real limitations as well as their capabilities. On the level of the human spirit, they let go of any illusions about life, and in an attitude of trust they affirm all that has been their lot, is their lot, and will be their lot in life. A positive adjustment to the middle age crisis becomes easier if the person has a good friend or counselor who can help him. The best helper would be someone whose solid judgment is based on his own life experience, someone who can stand by with empathy and sympathy. Such a helper will respect the action of nature and grace at this stage of the life cycle, and will encourage the middle aged person to face his own frailty, doubts, and anxiety about the future, since such feelings are normal at this phase of life. Together they will be able to make some sense out of the middle age crisis of limits and turn it into an opportunity for growth in wisdom, maturity, and grace.

Reflection

The middle age crisis is neither uncommon nor abnormal, but it can be a desert experience for the one going through it. A person's relationship with God, which might be thought to provide a firm support in such a crisis, is instead part of the crisis. As middle age corresponds chronologically to the time of mature adulthood, it challenges a person to achieve a grown-up, adult stage of the spiritual life. Adult faith is virile and realistic, giving of itself in service of others, honoring commitments, and listening for a word from the Lord in the circumstances of each new situation.

The desert experience is a proving ground for adult faith. In the desert of middle age I feel life has dealt too harshly with me and I am tempted to withdraw from the battle and lick my wounds, or seek new sources of consolation in an infantile wish for a life of blissful peace. The desert experience of inner emptiness and desertedness throws me back once again, in middle age, on my own basic poverty and my need to be saved by a power outside myself. God uses this experience to teach me that it is by his favor and not by my own unaided powers that I always have enough to live on.

When I look back over my life from the perspective of middle age, I may say that I have always tried to be faithful to what seemed right, although subsequent events have proved me wrong at times. But my fidelity to the light has now led me to another crisis, another desert experience. I am tired of deserts and tired of trusting in promises that are never fulfilled. It seems humanly impossible for me to go beyond this point.

The desert experience of middle age exhausts human possibilities and forces me either to despair or to rise to a new level of trust in divine possibilities. Again I face the choice of resisting the desert, yielding to it in despair, or accepting it with a stronger act of trusting faith. There are no heroics involved in these options; there is only the discovery of my own poverty and of God's unlimited mercy. If at this point I determine to stick it out where I am, and continue doing whatever I can for love of God and by his grace, then I open myself to a deeper sharing in the paschal mystery of Christ, dying with him and rising to life again with him. To continue on now, in this desert, will be to commit myself to a new beginning, with a new vision of hope.[2]

In a sense everything will change, but in another sense nothing will change except me. Life will remain externally the same as it always has been, and for me that means more of the same in the desert of the monastery, but my vision and my commitment will be new. I am coming of age and gaining a deeper perspective on life. This stage of maturity at the conclusion of the middle age crisis is described by French theologian Yves Congar:

> The worth of things is understood and the states of mind that have real significance; the significance of standing faithfully at one's post without distinction, of being silent, of really doing one's job, even of being misunderstood; the importance, the greatness, of little things, of realities that may not glitter but abide. What is worthwhile seems less exciting, and yet clearer and more enduring.[3]

So I go on being what I am and doing what has to be done in my monastic desert, but with a lighter and more carefree heart than I have had in years. I stop taking myself so seriously. I want to celebrate life as long as I can and as much as I can. I want to enjoy the beauty of the mountains and the blue sky, the refreshment of a walk in the morning coolness, the sound of birds singing and the laughter of my brothers, the smell of fresh bread cooling and of newly cut grass. I want to appreciate, as long as I can, the stimulation of a good discussion, an engrossing book, a rich and reverent liturgy. I resolve to live in grateful presence in the desert of my life. My middle age crisis proves to be a blessing in disguise.

PART B

THE DESERT OF SUFFERING AND DEATH

Acceptance of the desert experience meets its final test when I accept a desert death. In the Old Testament Moses entered the desert with courageous hope, marching through the parted sea, a song of triumph on his lips:

I will sing to the Lord for he is gloriously triumphant:
Horse and rider he has hurled into the sea.
The Lord is my strength and my song, for he has saved
  me! [Ex 15:1-2]

But in the course of his forty year desert experience Moses sinned against the Lord, and was punished by being forbidden to enter the promised land. He saw the land from a distance, but died without setting foot in it [Dt 32:52].

There are times in the course of a person's life when he feels that he too may die without ever setting foot in the promised land. Sickness and suffering, and especially the contracting of a terminal disease, are a desert experience in themselves. In suffering and death I experience all objects of my life-world falling away from me, as if I were being emptied out into nothingness; the moment of death appears to be a plunge into nothingness itself, in total aloneness. Suffering and death put my future in question, and therefore also my present and my whole self.[4] The response I make to this experience may be destructive and growth-inhibiting, or creative and growth-promoting.

Growth-inhibiting responses. Initially I may try to belittle the seriousness of my suffering or indulge in vain hope for a cure, telling myself that everything will be okay again very soon. But the day will come when I can no longer ignore the criticalness of my situation. If I am quick tempered, I am likely to become bitterly resentful and angry, lashing out at those around me, at life in general, and even at God. I may rebel against the way God has chosen to treat me after I have served him so faithfully. I may attempt to bargain with God and promise him anything if only he will spare me. If this gambit fails I may feel completely crushed, and allow myself to sink into a deep depression and despair.[5]

Growth-promoting responses. It may be necessary to try some or all of the growth-inhibiting responses before I see the futility of such an attitude. I cannot effectively say No to the desert experience of suffering and death; we all die. But by saying Yes to the necessity of death I can transcend that necessity and make it subject to my will; what I freely accept is no longer imposed on me even though I have no choice but to die someday. By freely saying Yes I give meaning to what I am going through and turn my fate into a personal decision. Of my own accord I can reach out and take hold of the destiny being thrust into my hand.

With the ever-present help of divine grace I can do more. I can accept my desert experience of suffering and death out of obedience to the God who wills it for some inscrutable but loving reason of his own. Grace inspires me to a self-surrendering acceptance of something I cannot understand or explain, a desert death. Instead of trying to change the inevitable, I gently let go of my desire to be in control of my life and my future. I am free to dispose of myself in an act of creative acceptance, in faith and trust.

My faith attains its most explicit Christian expression when I accept death in the desert as a participation in the paschal mystery of the death and resurrection of Jesus. If I am told that cancer has been found in me and major surgery is necessary immediately, I can still give voice to the cry that tries to surface: "O God, why me?" But as soon as I say it, I think of a similar cry that rose from the heart of my dying savior. In the words of Jürgen Moltmann, German theologian:

> Anyone who suffers without cause first thinks that he has been forsaken by God. God seems to him to be the mysterious, incomprehensible God who destroys the good fortune that he gave. But anyone who cries out to God in this suffering echoes the death-cry of the dying Christ, the son of God.[6]

In union with the dying Christ I can look straight into the face of suffering, death, and the desert experience and fully accept these consequences of my finitude and mortality, fully subject myself to the incomprehensible but loving providence of God my father. At that moment of acceptance of God's will for me, I find a serene joy. I should be able to say of every illness that afflicts me or my loved ones what Jesus himself said of the final illness of Lazarus: "This sickness . . . is for God's glory" [Jn 11:4]. In faith and trust I understand the ultimate meaning of my desert experience as a graced participation in the passion and death of Jesus, with the hope of participating also in his glorious resurrection.

PART C

THROUGH THE DESERT WITH CHEERFUL TRUST

Thomas Merton has written that *"Alleluia* is the song of the desert."[7] Alleluia is the song of paschal triumph and joy. The desertedness and inner emptiness of the desert may not entirely disappear, but because of the miracle of the paschal mystery, that emptiness can coexist in a person's heart along with a deep peace, a sense of humor, a compassionate love, and a transforming hope and joy in the risen Christ. In the paschal mystery death is changed into life and man is restored to the friendship with God enjoyed by Adam in the primordial garden of Eden. When a person responds to the desert experience in creative acceptance, his heart becomes a garden where God once again walks with man. In this section we will survey a theme from scripture about the desert blooming and the arid wastes being transformed into a new paradise. This theme is the basis of cheerful trust and the song of Alleluia in the midst of the desert experience.

The Desert Blooms

I remember how surprised I was to come upon flowers blooming in the Arizona desert in the month of August. I knew that flowers are abundant in the spring, after the rainy season, but I thought everything would be burnt dry by August. Yet, in those impossible conditions of heat and dryness, the sand verbena was in full bloom. There were other varieties too, not many and not large, but they were flowers in the desert. I had no idea where they found water and nourishment in that lifeless sand. Their tiny petals, pink and white and yellow, were a vivid symbol of life in a land where life has supposedly given up the struggle to survive. Their delicate presence transformed harshness into beauty.[8]

I thought of the Old Testament prophecies that described the Messianic era as an age when the wasteland would become a fertile plain crossed by fresh streams, abundant with grain and trees and flowers. On that day God would accomplish "a new thing" on earth, a deed more marvelous than the exodus from Egypt, a mighty intervention in human history that would transform the face of the earth. The effects of Messiah's coming would be like rivers opening in the desert for the chosen people to drink from [Is 43:19-21; 35:7; Jer 31:9; Ps 107:34]. Friendship would be reestablished between God and man:

> On every bare height shall their pastures be.
> They shall not hunger or thirst,
> Nor shall the scorching wind or the sun strike them;
> For he who pities them leads them
> And guides them beside springs of water [Is 49:10].

The long desert experience of God's people will come to an end as the desert is changed into a verdant grove of trees. God promises:

> I will make the wilderness a pool,
> And the parched land fountains of water,
> I will turn the desert into a marshland,
> And the dry ground into springs of water.
> I will plant in the desert the cedar,
> Acacia, myrtle, and olive;

I will set in the wasteland the cypress,
Together with the plane tree and the pine,
That all may see and know,
Observe and understand,
That the hand of the Lord has done this,
The Holy One of Israel has created it [Is 41:18-20].

Israel has only to allow the hand of the Lord room to act and believe that his creative power can accomplish this marvel. What is impossible for man, God will accomplish. Then Israel will rejoice, and the desert itself will bloom:

The desert and the parched land will exult;
The steppe will rejoice and bloom.
They will bloom with abundant flowers.
And rejoice with joyful song [Is 35:1-2].

When the lily appears on the desert sand it will be the sign of new life, the sign of resurrection and victory over death [Ct 2:11-12].

In the New Testament we have seen that the wilderness theme has an important theological function in Mark's gospel. When Mark narrates the feeding of the five thousand, he presents the miracle as the messianic metamorphosis of the desert into a land of refreshment and beauty. Twice Mark reminds us that the feeding takes place "in a deserted place" [Mk 6:32, 35]. Yet there is green grass in this desert, and the suggestion of flower beds formed by the colorful garments of the crowd: "The people took their places in hundreds and fifties, neatly arranged like flower beds" [Mk 6:40]. The desert has become a place of beauty, a fertile plain where the followers of Jesus may rest and be fed by him as a shepherd feeds his flock. With a few, carefully selected phrases, Mark hints that the prophecies of old are now being fulfilled by the presence and power of Jesus.⁹ The desert has become an Eden at the beginning of a new creation.

Return to Paradise

The new creation, accomplished through the life, death, and resurrection of Jesus, has sometimes been described by monastic spirituality as a return to the original, paradisal condition of man before the fall. Genesis describes the human situation as God first intended it [Gen 2:8-10]:

> The Lord God planted a garden in Eden, in the east, and he placed there the man whom he had formed. Out of the ground the Lord God made various trees grow that were delightful to look at and good for food, . . . A river rises in Eden to water the garden.

In the garden man enjoyed intimacy with God [Gen 3:8]. But that relationship was destroyed by disobedience, and man was expelled from the garden of Eden. The land itself was cursed with infertility, destined to produce only "thorns and thistles" [Gen 3:18]. The cursed land, from which man himself had been taken, was the image of man's spiritual condition of disobedience. The human heart was like an arid, sterile desert because of sin.

The goal of monastic life was to recover the paradisal state of intimacy with God. The monk's heart had to be washed pure and clean by the tears of compunction, and thus be transformed from a desert into a garden: "You will be like a well watered garden" [Is 53:11]. In that garden the monk would encounter his creator and walk with him in intimacy and loving trust, as Adam walked with God in Eden [Ct 4:12]. The first monks chose the physical desert as the shortest and surest path to that paradise of the heart in which man walks in harmonious unity with God, with his neighbor, and with himself. Purity, simplicity, and oneness of heart were signs of the return to paradise. The multitude of hermits and cenobites that dotted the deserts of Egypt and Palestine appeared to St. Jerome's literary imagination as flowers springing up in the desert sand, and he wrote: "O desert of Christ, burgeoning with flowers! . . . O wilderness rejoicing in intimacy with God."[10] Thus the monks transformed both the physical desert and the desert of the human heart by patiently and simply cooperating with the creative work of transformation being accomplished by the power of the Lord of the desert. As the desert experience of their own poverty assimilated them to the death of Jesus, to that degree the desert of their hearts bloomed by the power of his resurrection.

Reflection

The desert experience, creatively accepted, opens on to the joy of emptiness and nothingness in the face of God's infinite, loving goodness. The desert can become the instrument of transformation through which a person's humanity is expanded, deepened, enriched, and divinized. The path that leads through the desert can lead also to inner freedom, peace, love, and joy. The more the desert experience is accepted in living trust, the more securely do we rest in the embrace of God's mercy, discovering ever new and unexpected depths within it. Joy is the spontaneous expression of gratefulness for God's merciful care on the journey through the desert. I am thinking of one joyful brother in my community who habitually greets you with a cheerful smile as you pass and frequently flashes the sign for"Beautiful!" The Trappist sign language is limited when it comes to expressing moods and feelings, but this sign is Brother's way of saying, "Everything's peachy, there's nothing to worry about, it's all in good hands, have a happy day, have a happy life!" Such joy, completely spontaneous and sincere, can be characteristic of anybody's life even in the desert.[11]

Joy in the desert is not like the feeling of euphoria that may come from God's felt nearness in times of consolation. Desert joy is the joy of those who have nothing of their own but expect all things from the one in whom they have placed their trust. Their poverty includes the lack of spiritual lights and satisfactions and special charisms. Such gifts are not to be despised if God grants them, but there can be a joyful service of God without them. St. John of the Cross wrote the following to Donna Juana de Pedraza who was traveling by a desert path and did not know whether she could be joyful about it or not:

> You were never better off than now, because you were never so humble nor so submissive. . . . And if one does not err in this, what need is there in order to be right other than to walk along the level road of the law of God and of the Church and live only in dark and true faith and certain hope and complete charity, expecting all our blessings in heaven, living here below like pilgrims, the poor, the exiled, orphans, the thirsty, without a road and without anything, hoping for everything in heaven.[12]

The desert pilgrim hopes for everything in the promised land. Because his hope is certain, his joy is full. He walks under the watchful gaze of a heavenly Father whose presence, though unseen and unfelt, surrounds and envelopes him with constant, loving care. He journeys through the desert but his heart rests already in the promised land.

Conclusion

At the end of this study of the desert experience we have learned a simple lesson: living trust in the Lord of the desert is the secret of surviving and even of flourishing in the desert. God is sovereignly free to lead us to himself by any way he pleases, whether through a desert or beside restful waters. Living trust is confident that, by whatever path, God always leads his people to himself.

The limited purpose of this book has made it necessary to concentrate on the desert path rather than on the final goal of the journey, which is the promised land of God. I have chosen to study the purifying desert experience without much reference to that for which the desert purifies us—a life of beatifying intimacy with God that can begin already on this earth. But the trials of the desert journey should never make us forget the journey's end. As we trudge through the dust of our desert days, we need to keep in mind the splendid promises of scripture:

> The Lord your God is bringing you into a good country, a land with streams of water, with springs and fountains welling up in the hills and valleys, a land of wheat and barley, of vines and fig trees and pomegranates, of olive trees and of honey, a land where you can eat bread without stint and where you will want nothing [Dt 8:8-9].

The promised land, brimming with delights, is a scriptural metaphor for God himself and for the transfigured existence of man with God. God draws us, through the desert of this life, to himself. He stands at the far side of the desert experience, as the risen Jesus stood in the dawn light on the shore of the Sea of Tiberias [Jn 21:4]. Like the disciples in the boat, we toil in the waves of a sea of desert sand, trying to reach the shore of that good country where the risen Lord calls us to come and eat of his meal and never be empty again. Slowly the disciples made their way to Jesus, and perhaps the way seemed arduous to them at times, but "actually they were not far from shore" [Jn 21:8].

FOOTNOTES

PART I

CHAPTER I

1. Thomas Merton, *The Sign of Jonas* (New York: Harcourt, Brace and Co., 1953), 34-35, entry of March 30, 1947.

2. Thomas Merton, *New Seeds of Contemplation* (New York: New Directions, 1961), 250.

3. Compare the story of the Mohammedan mystic in Nikos Kazantzakis, *Report to Greco,* trans. P.A. Bien (New York: Bantam Books, 1966), 448.

4. Ralph Greenson, "On Boredom," *Journal of American Psychoanalytic Association* 1 (1953), 17. I have used Greenson's research in my description of boredom. See also his article, "The Psychology of Apathy," *Psychoanalytic Quarterly* 18 (1949), 290-302.

CHAPTER II

1. Michel Siffre, "Six Months Alone in a Cave," *National Geographic,* Vol. 147, No. 3 (March, 1975), 426-435. All quotations from this article will be followed immediately by their page number in brackets.

2. Henry G. Bugbee, "Loneliness, Solitude and the Twofold Way in which Concern seems to be Claimed," *Humanitas* Vol. X, No. 3 (November, 1974), 313. This entire issue of *Humanitas* studies the topic of loneliness.

3. Clark Moustakas, *Loneliness* (Englewood Cliffs, New Jersey: Prentice-Hall, 1961), 2-3.

4. James J. Lynch, *The Broken Heart* (New York: Basic Books, 1977).

5. There does exist, however, a considerable literature on loneliness, mostly by psychologists. See the bibliography in *Humanitas* X, 3 (November, 1974). See also Sister Gertrude Mulholland, "Spirituality and Living With Loneliness" (Unpublished Master's thesis, Center for the Study of Spirituality of the Institute of Man, Duquesne University, Pittsburgh, 1976).

6. Simone Weil, *Gravity and Grace* (London: Routledge and Kegan Paul, 1963), 34.

CHAPTER III

1. On this point and on meaning and meaninglessness in general, see Peter Berger, *The Sacred Canopy* (Garden City, New York: Doubleday, 1969), and also Peter Berger and Thomas Luckman, *The Social Construction of Reality* (Garden City, New York: Doubleday, 1966), 21, 23, 35.

2. Paul Tillich, *The Courage To Be* (New Haven, Connecticut: Yale University Press, 1952), 176.

3. Albert Camus, *The Plague,* trans. Stuart Gilbert (New York: Alfred Knopf, 1969). Direct quotations from *The Plague* will be followed immediately by a page reference to the above edition. See the commentary by Thomas Merton, "Albert Camus" "The Plague": Introduction and Commentary, Religious Dimensions in Literature Series (New York: Seabury Press, 1968).

4. Jurgen Moltmann, *The Crucified God* (New York: Harper and Row, 1974), 338.

5. T.S. Eliot, "Choruses from 'The Rock,' " *The Complete Poems and Plays 1909-1950* (New York: Harcourt, Brace and World, 1971), 98.

CHAPTER IV

1. Adrian van Kaam, *The Dynamics of Spiritual Self Direction* (Denville, New Jersey: Dimension Books, 1976), 65-71.

2. For a description sensitive to the desert-experience implications of the Elijah story see: Jean D'Arc, "Elie et nous," *La Vie Spirituelle* No. 377 (Octobre, 1952), 289-295.

3. See Augustine Stock, *The Way in the Wilderness: Exodus, Wilderness and Moses Themes in Old Testament and New* (Collegeville, Minnesota: Liturgical Press, 1969), 62-63.

4. See Jean Steinmann, *Saint John the Baptist and the Desert Tradition* (New York: Harper and Brothers, 1958).

5. We should have a rather broad concept even of the geographical desert: "The adjective 'deserted' and the substantive 'desert' refer to 'abandonment,' whether of a person, or a cause, or a locality. The latter does not have to be a desert. It is a place 'without inhabitants,' 'empty,' e.g. an 'abandoned city' or a 'thinly populated district.' It can naturally mean 'waste' in the strict sense, e.g. an unprofitable 'waste of stone and sand' and it can thus be used for a 'lonely' heath (e.g. Lk 15:4 where the shepherd leaves the ninety-nine sheep 'in the desert'). Gerhard Kittel, ed., *Theological Dictionary of the New Testament,* trans. and ed. Geoffrey W. Bromiley, Vol. II (Grand Rapids: Eerdmans, 1964), 657. Thus the biblical "desert" can refer to "sparsely populated, barren plains which, however, provide enough pasturage for herds," see Ulrich W. Mauser, *Christ in the Wilderness* (London: SCM Press Ltd., 1963), 18.

6. Thomas Merton, "Wilderness and Paradise," *Cistercian Studies* Vol. IV, No. 1 (1967), 85.

7. Walter Brueggemann, *The Land* (Philadelphia: Fortress, 1977), 42.

8. George H. Williams can speak of "the fascinatingly am-

bivalent character of the primordial desert motif in the Old Testament." *Wilderness and Paradise in Christian Thought* (New York: Harper, 1962), 7. See pp. 5 and 15 for further scriptural references.

9. The term is Thomas Merton's in *Disputed Questions* (New York: Ferrar, Straus & Cudahy, 1960), 224.

10. Demetrius Dumm, "Monasticism and Contemporary Culture," *American Benedictine Review* 26:2 (June, 1975), 133.

11. Interpretations given in this section rely on Ulrich Mauser's study of the desert theme in the gospel of Mark, in his book: *Christ in the Wilderness*, Studies in Biblical Theology #39 (London: SCM Press Ltd., 1963). See especially pp. 98-99, 107, 117, 123, 132. Mauser says: "Of all the side themes of the wilderness tradition, both in the Old and New Testament, [temptation] is the most frequent one" [p. 99].

12. See Pierre Bonnard, "La Signification du desert selon le Nouveau Testament," *Hommage et Reconnaissance,* Recueil de traveaux publiés a l'occasion du soixantième anniversaire de Karl Barth, Cahiers Théologiques de l'Actualité Protestante (Paris: Neuchatel, 1946), 12.

13. The gospel of John does not describe an agony in the garden, but the desert feeling of aloneness, sorrow, and dread, is apparent when Jesus says: "My soul is troubled now, yet what should I say—Father, save me from this hour? But it was for this that I came to this hour" [Jn 12:27, with a possible allusion to Ps 6:4].

14. Augustine Stock, *The Way in the Wilderness* (Collegeville, Minnesota: The Liturgical Press, 1969), 117.

15. An early thirteenth century monastic author, possibly Helinand of Froidmont, commented on the "*Eli, Eli*" cry of Jesus and wrote: "Truly the cross of Christ is called a desert because it is inhabited by few, and Christ our God is a true her-

mit by whom the cross is carried." Quoted in the *Instruction on the Contemplative Life and on the Enclosure of Nuns,* Congregation for Religious, August 15, 1969 (United States Catholic Conference Publication), p. 15, n. 11.

16. Xavier Léon-Dufour, *Dictionary of Biblical Theology* (2nd rev. ed.; New York; Seabury Press, 1973), 123.

CHAPTER V

1. For this explanation of temptation see Xavier Léon-Dufour, *Dictionary of Biblical Theology* (2nd rev. ed.; New York: Seabury Press, 1973), 615, 617.

2. St. Athanasius, *The Life of Saint Antony,* ed. and trans. Robert T. Meyer, Ancient Christian Writers, No. 10 (Westminster, Maryland: The Newman Press. 1950), 29.

3. See Paul Evdokimov, *The Struggle with God* (Glen Rock, New Jersey: Paulist Press, 1966), 102.

4. See René Voillaume, "In the Desert With Our Lord," *Jesus Caritas* No. 29 (Summer, 1974), 7.

5. Nikos Kazantzakis, going through a desert experience at the monastery of St. Catherine on Mount Sinai, wrote: "Within me were the dark, immemorial forces of the Evil One, human and prehuman; within me too were the luminous forces, human and prehuman, of God—and my soul was the arena where these two armies clashed and met." *Report to Greco,* trans. P. A. Bien (New York: Bantam Books, 1966), 277.

6. Quoted by Thomas Aquinas, *Summa Theologiae,* III/41/2 ad 2. The text is from a spurious work attributed to St. John Chrysostom, the *Fifth Homily on Matthew.*

7. See this theme developed by Carl J. Pfeifer, "Wandering

Through the Desert in Our Hearts," *Worcester Free Press,* October 10, 1975.

8. The idea of temptation as an identity experience is developed by George Aschenbrenner, "Hidden in Jesus Before the Father," *Review for Religious* Vol. 34, No. 1 (January, 1975), 126.

9. *The Collected Works of Saint John of the Cross,* trans. Kieran Kavanaugh and Otilio Rodriguez (Washington, D.C.: Institute of Carmelite Studies Publications, 1973), 375.

10. Nikos Kazantzakis, *Report to Greco,* trans. P. A. Bien (New York: Bantam Books, 1966), 349.

11. Carlo Carretto, *Letters From the Desert* (Maryknoll, New York: Orbis Books, 1972), xviii-xix.

12. St. John of the Cross makes good use of the metaphor of weaning as he comments on a verse from Isaiah:
" 'Whom shall God teach His knowledge? And to whom shall He explain His message? To them that are weaned, from the milk, and to them who are drawn away from the breasts' [Is 28:9]. This passage indicates that the preparation for this divine influx is not the former milk of spiritual sweetness, nor aid from the breast of the discursive meditations of the sensory faculties which the soul enjoyed, but the privation of the one and a withdrawal from the other." *The Collected Works of St. John of the Cross,* 323. See also: 1 Cor 3:1-2.

13. See Thomas Merton, *Contemplation in a World of Action* (New York: Image Books, 1973), 242. Cf St. Jerome's letter to Heliodorus which includes the phrase, "the desert loves to strip bare" ["*nudos amat eremus*"—Ep., xiv 1:3].

14. "We must be ready to be dismantled over and over again, until we are entirely remade, receiving our likeness to God from God himself, not trying to seize it for ourselves. . . ." Simon

Tugwell, *Prayer, Keeping Company With God* (Dublin: Veritas Publications, 1974), Vol. I, p. 42.

15. *The Collected Works of St. John of the Cross,* op. cit., 669.

16. Thomas Merton, *The Climate of Monastic Prayer* (Spencer, Massachusetts: Cistercian Publications, 1969), 121. This work was also published with the title *Contemplative Prayer* (New York: Herder and Herder, 1969).

17. See Susan Annette Muto, "Solitude, Self-Presence and True Participation," *Spiritual Life* Vol. 20 (Winter, 1974), 235.

18. See William McNamara, "The Desert," *Desert Call,* May, 1971, 42-43.

19. To mention only a few such centers currently available, there is the Lebh Shomea House of Prayer (Sarita, Texas), and the Spiritual Life Institute with houses at Nada Ranch (Sedona, Arizona) and Nova Nada (Kemptville, Nova Scotia).

20. In the document on the *Spiritual Renewal of the American Priesthood* [eds. Ernest Larkin and Gerald Broccolo (Washington, D.C.: USCC Publications, 1973), p. 69] diocesan priests are encouraged to set aside time in their busy schedules for an occasional "day in the desert." We read:
"Many priests have found their personal encounter with the Lord facilitated by a 'desert experience' or a 'Day in the Desert.' This can take the form of a full day each month, or at least four to six hours spent alone, without work to get done, without props to fill the time, in the countryside, at a river, in long walks, or even in an empty room. It is a day lived solely for Christ with the time devoted only to him, 'wasted,' as it were, with him."

21. *Raïssa's Journal,* ed. Jacques Maritain (Albany, New York: Magi Books, 1974). All quotations from this book will be followed by the page reference in brackets.

22. *The Collected Works of St. John of the Cross,* op. cit., 347.

23. Thomas Merton, *The Climate of Monastic Prayer,* 121. In *New Seeds of Contemplation* (New York: New Directions, 1961), 235, Merton reminds us that "the ordinary way to contemplation lies through a desert without trees and without beauty and without water." The prospect of this desert so appalls most people that they "cannot believe that contemplation and sanctity are to be found in a desolation where there is no food for their imagination and intellect and for the desires of their nature."

24. *The Collected Works of St. John of the Cross,* 323. On the thirst for God in the longing of love that is fostered by the desert experience of aridity in prayer, see p. 319. St. John does not hesitate to say elsewhere that this experience of dryness and darkness is beneficial: " . . . it is fitting that the soul be brought into emptiness and poverty and abandonment in all its parts and left in dryness and darkness" [p. 339].

25. Thomas Merton, *The Climate of Monastic Prayer,* 147.

26. *The Collected Works of St. John of the Cross,* 334.

27. *The Collected Works of St. John of the Cross,* 338. Rejection is not, however, the only affliction. There are others, comparable to the sufferings of purgatory or hell (see pp. 338-357). A fine commentary may be found in Georges Morel, *Le Sens de L'Existence Selon S. Jean de la Croix* (Paris: Aubier, 1961), Vol, III, p. 88ff.

See also the article "Déréliction" by Henri Martin in the *Dictionaire de Spiritualité* in which he describes this desert as "a lived communion with the state of abandonment by God of Christ on the cross' [col. 511]. Related articles may be found in the *Dictionaire* under "Aridité," "Dégoût," "Désolation."

28. See Augustine F. Baker, *Holy Wisdom or Directions for*

the Prayer of Contemplation, ed. from the Douay edition of 1657 by Abbot Sweeney (London: Burns, Oates & Washbourne, 1950), 538-539 [Sec. IV, ch. V].

29. On the presence of God in his absence, see also: St. John of the Cross *The Spiritual Canticle,* Stanza 1, No. 4, *Collected Works,* p. 417; José Ortega y Gasset, *Man and People,* trans. Willard Trask (New York: W. W. Norton, 1963), 100; Denis Vasse, *Le Temps du Desir* (Paris: Editions du Seuil, 1969), 42; Simone Weil, *Gravity and Grace* (London: Routledge, 1952), 99.

CHAPTER VI

1. See Adrian van Kaam, *In Search of Spiritual Identity* (Denville, New Jersey: Dimension Books, 1975), 186.

2. A fine survey of positive and growth-promotive responses to the Christian desert experience, together with suggested scriptural and non-scriptural readings, may be found in: Susan Annette Muto, *A Practical Guide to Spiritual Reading* (Denville, New Jersey: Dimension Books, 1976), 58-95. See especially Minor Theme VII, on "Trust and Dependence in Desert Experience," pp. 80-84.

3. Jürgen Moltmann, *The Crucified God* (New York: Harper and Row, 1974), 276. Cf. Rom 8:31; 2 Cor 5:21; Gal 3:13.

4. Louis Chardon, *The Cross of Jesus,* trans. Richard Murphy (St. Louis: Herder, 1957), Vol. I, p. 295.

5. St. John of the Cross comments on the extent of Jesus' abandonment:
"At the moment of His death He was certainly annihilated in His soul, without any consolation or relief, since the Father left

Him that way in innermost aridity in the lower part. He was thereby compelled to cry out: 'My God, my God, why have You forsaken me?' This was the most extreme abandonment, sensitively, that He had suffered in His life. And by it He accomplished the most marvelous work of His whole life, surpassing all the works and deeds and miracles that He had ever performed on earth or in heaven. That is, He brought about the reconciliation and union of the human race with God through grace. The Lord achieved this, as I say, at the moment in which He was most annihilated in all things: in His reputation before men, since in beholding Him die they mocked Him instead of esteeming Him; in His human nature, by dying; and in spiritual help and consolation from His Father, for He was forsaken by His Father at that time so as to pay the debt fully and bring man to union with God. David says of Him: *Ad nihilum redactus sum et nescivi* [I was brought to nothing and did not understand—Ps 72:22]. . . . When [the Christian] is brought to nothing, the highest degree of humility, the spiritual union between his soul and God will be effected. This union is the most noble and sublime state attainable in this life. The journey, then, does not consist in recreations, experiences, and spiritual feelings, but in the living, sensory and spiritual, exterior and interior death of the cross." *The Collected Works of St. John of the Cross,* trans. Kieran Kavanaugh and Otilio Rodriguez (Washington, D.C.: Institute of Carmelite Studies Publications, 1973), 124-125.

6. In a striking formula, Paul Tillich speaks of: " . . . the Church which preaches the Crucified who cried to God who remained his God after the God of confidence had left him in the darkness of doubt and meaninglessness." *The Courage to Be* (New Haven: Yale University Press, 1952), 188.

7. This reflection is based in part on Karl Rahner, *Opportunities for Faith,* trans. Edwin Quinn (New York: Seabury Press, 1974), 34, 39, 138; and *Watch and Pray With Me,* trans. William Dych (New York: Herder and HJerder, 1966), 51-52.

8. Two of the saints who went through desert experiences of aridity and temptation lasting for decades and decades are St. Jane de Chantal and St. Alphonsus. See Vital Lehodey, *Holy Abandonment,* trans. Ailbe Luddy (Dublin: M.H. Gill and Son, 1948)l, 406-407, 410-411.

9. Jean-Pierre de Caussade, *Abandonment to Divine Providence,* trans. R. J. Strickland (Exeter, England: Sydney Lee, 1921), 113.

10. Notable also is de Caussade's letter to a nun, p. 348:
"I greatly approve, my dear Sister, of the patience with which you endure the great emptiness you experience in your soul. By this you will make more progress in one month than you would in several years of sweetness and consolation. About this I can only exhort you to go on in the same way. It is necessary to traverse this desert to reach during this life the promised land. I am not at all surprised that this great emptiness seems like a support to you. This is what, in fact, it is, because God is present therein, but in an almost imperceptible manner, just as He was in your trials. Look upon this distaste for all things, and apparent want of feeling towards all that is not God, as a great grace to be carefully guarded and preserved. God will come at the time fixed by His grace to fill the void which He has made in your heart. . . .'"

11. Walter J. Ciszek with Daniel Flaherty, *He Leadeth Me* (Garden City, New York: Doubleday, 1973), 77.

12. Augustine Baker remarks, "What has a soul left to fear that can with a peaceable mind support, yea, and make her benefit of the absence of God himself?" *Holy Wisdom,* ed. Abbot Sweeney (London: Burns, Oates & Washbourne, 1950), 541.

13. Thus St. Francis de Sales can advise someone:
". . . remain indifferent to deliverance from your spiritual desolation. This does not mean that you may not *wish* for this deliverance, but you must not *set your heart* on it. We must

resign ourselves to God's merciful providence in our regard, prepared to serve him in the midst of these desert thorns as long as it pleases him. . . . If we cannot offer our Lord a devotion that is sweet let us offer him one that is dry, for it is all one to him so long as we are firmly resolved to love him." *Introduction to the Devout Life,* trans. Michael Day (New York: E.P. Dutton, 1961), 232; see also 223.

CHAPTER VII

1. The following synthesis of psychological theory on the middle age crisis is based on these sources: Nicholas Ayo, "Middle Age and Spiritual Growth," *Cross and Crown,* Vol. 25 (1973), 238-245; Bernard Basset, *The Noonday Devil* (New York: Image Books, 1964); George Devine, "The Mid-Life Crisis" *National Catholic Reporter,* November 8, 1974, pp. 7-14; Erik Erikson, "The Problem of Ego Identity," *Psychological Issues,* Vol. I, No. 1 (1959); Barbara Fried, *The Middle-Age Crisis* (New York: Harper and Row, 1976); Margaret Hellie Huyck, *Growing Older* (Englewood Cliffs, New Jersey: Prentice Hall, 1974); Carl Gustav Jung, *Modern Man in Search of a Soul* (New York: Harcourt, Brace and World, 1933); William F. Kraft, *The Psychology of Nothingness* (Philadelphia: Westminster Press, 1974); M. Albert Lassus, "Forty—The Difficult Age" *Cistercian Studies* Vol. 4, No. 3 (1969), 226-233; Eda LeShan, *The Wonderful Crisis of Middle Age* (New York: Warner Paperback, 1974); Barry McLoughlin, *Nature, Grace and Religious Development* (Westminster, Maryland: Newman, 1965); Fred McMorrow, "Men and Midolescence," *The Pittsburgh Press,* February 2, 1975, p. 5 (adapted from *Midolescence: The Dangerous Years* (Quadrangle Books, 1974); Bernice Neugarten, ed., *Personality in Middle and Late Life* (New York: Prentice-Hall, 1964); Leslie Tizard and Harry Guntrip, *Middle Age* (Great Neck Long Island, New York: Channel Press, 1960).

2. See an elaboration of this alternative in Rene Voillaume, *Brothers of Men* (Baltimore: Helicon, 1966), 30-32.

3. Yves Congar, *Faith and Spiritual Life,* trans. A. Manson and L. C. Sheppard (New York: Herder and Herder, 1968), 153.
Compare William Kraft's description of the "gentle, mild and gracious" person who has come successfully through a middle age crisis of limits: *A Psychology of Nothingness* (Philadelphia: Westminster Press, 1974), 110.

4. The thoughts on suffering and death developed in this section are based on lectures given by Adrian van Kaam during the spring semester, 1977, at Duquesne University. Unauthorized publication of this material is unethical.

5. On the stages of dying, see Elisabeth Kübler-Ross, *On Death and Dying* (New York: Macmillan, 1969), 38-111.

6. Jürgen Moltmann, *The Crucified God* (New York: Harper and Row, 1974), 252.

7. Thomas Merton, *The Climate of Monastic Prayer* (Spencer, Massachusetts: Cistercian Publications, 1969), 34.

8. Photographs of the desert in bloom may be seen in *Arizona Highways,* April, 1976. For complete botannical descriptions see Edmund Jaeger, *Desert Wild Flowers* (Stanford, California: Stanford University Press, 1941). Jaeger writes: "Contrary to the usual opinion, there is not a month in the year when no plants are in flower in the desert" [p. ix].

9. Ulrich Mauser, *Christ in the Wilderness* (London: SCM Press, Ltd., 1963), 136-137.

10. St. Jerome, Ep. xiv:10. See G.J.M. Bartelnik, "Les oxymores *desertum civitas* et *desertum floribus vernans,*" *Studia Monastica,* Vol. 15, Fasc. 1 (1973), 7-16.

11. See the chapter "Is Joy Still Possible?" in Pius-Raymond

Régamey, *The Cross and the Christian,* trans. Angeline Bouchard (St. Louis: Herder Book Co., 1954), 158-177.

12. *The Collected Works of Saint John of the Cross,* trans. Kieran Kavanaugh and Otilio Rodriguez (Washington, D.C.: Institute of Carmelite Studies Publications, 1973), Letter 19, p. 699.

SELECTED BIBLIOGRAPHY

Athanasius, Saint. *The Life of Saint Antony.* Translated and edited by Robert T. Meyer. No. 10. *Ancient Christian Writers.* Westminster, Maryland, 1950.

Brueggemann, Walter. *The Land.* Philadelphia: Fortress, 1977.

Camus, Albert. *The Plague.* Trans. by Stuart Gilbert. New York: Alfred A. Knopf, 1969.

Ciszek, Walter J., with Daniel Flaherty. *He Leadeth Me.* Garden City, New York: Doubleday, 1973.

Congar, Yves. *Faith and Spiritual Life.* Translated by A. Manson and L.C. Sheppard. New York: Herder and Herder, 1968.

De Caussade, J.P. *Abandonment To Divine Providence.* Translated by E. J. Strickland. Exeter, England: Sydney Lee, 1921.

Fried, Barbara. *The Middle-Age Crisis.* Rev. ed. with new intro. by Robert Raines. New York: Harper & Row, 1976.

Gannon, Thomas M., and George W. Traub. *The Desert and the City.* London: Macmillan Company, 1969.

Guntrip, Harry. *Schizoid Phenomena, Object Relations and the Self.* New York: International Universities Press, 1969.

John of the Cross, Saint. *The Collected Works of Saint John of the Cross.* Translated by Kieran Kavanaugh and Otilio Rodriguez. Washington, D.C.: Institute of Carmelite Studies Publications, 1973.

Kübler-Ross, Elisabeth. *On Death and Dying.* New York: Macmillan, 1969.

Kraft, William F. *A Psychology of Nothingness.* Philadelphia: Westminster Press, 1974.

Léon-Dufour, Xavier, ed. *Dictionary of Biblical Theology.* 2nd rev. ed. New York: Seabury Press, 1973.

McKenzie, John L. *Vital Concepts of the Bible.* Wilkes-Barre, Pennsylvania: Dimension Books, 1967.

Maritain, Jacques, ed. *Raïssa's Journal.* Albany, New York: Magi Books, 1974.

Mauser, Ulrich W. *Christ in the Wilderness.* Vol. 39. *Studies in Biblical Theology.* London: SCM Press, Ltd., 1963.

Merton, Thomas. *The Climate of Monastic Prayer.* Spencer, Massachusetts: Cistercian Publications, 1969.

Moltmann, Jürgen. *The Crucified God.* New York: Harper and Row, 1974.

Moustakas, Clark. *Loneliness.* Englewood Cliffs, New Jersey: Prentice-Hall, 1961.

Muto, Susan. *A Practical Guide to Spiritual Reading.* Denville, New Jersey: Dimension Books, 1976.

Régamey, Pius-Raymond. *The Cross and the Christian.* Translated by Angeline Bouchard. St. Louis: Herder Book Co., 1954.

Steinmann, Jean. *Saint John the Baptist ana the Desert Tradition.* New York: Harper and Brothers, 1958.

Stock, Augustine. *The Way in the Wilderness.* Collegeville, Minnesota: Liturgical Press, 1969.

Tillich, Paul. *The Courage To Be.* New Haven, Connecticut: Yale University Press, 1952.

van Kaam, Adrian. *The Dynamics of Spiritual Self Direction.* Denville, New Jersey: Dimension Books, 1976.

Voillaume, Rene. *Brothers of Men.* Baltimore: Helicon, 1966.

Weil, Simone. *Gravity and Grace.* London: Routledge and Kegan Paul, 1963.

Williams, George H. *Wilderness and Paradise in Christian Thought.* New York: Harper, 1962.

Periodicals

Barron, Mary Catherine. "Prayer and the Desert," *Review for Religious* XXXIV:6 (November, 1975), 897-900.

Lassus, M.-Albert. "Forty—The Difficult Age," *Cistercian Studies* IV:3 (1969), 226-233.

Greenson, Ralph R. "On Boredon," *Journal of American Psychoanalytic Association* I (1953), 7-21.

McNamara, William. "Desert Experience," *New Catholic World,* April 1974, 89-93.

Siffre, Michel. "Six Months Alone in a Cave," *National Geographic* 147:3 (March, 1975), 426-435.

Worden, Thomas. "The Presence and Absence of God," *Jesus Caritas,* No. 33 (Summer, 1975), 13-20.